W9-DGZ-227

Men of
GOD

by
Nina P. Ross

Nina P. Ross

Emmanuel Ministries Press

Men of God © Copyright 2005, Emmanuel Ministries Press

Published in the U.S.A. by Emmanuel Ministries Press

Scripture quotations are from the authorized King James Version.

Book cover and text design by BookSetters, Bowling Green, KY.

Edited by Trent Booker.

Library of Congress Cataloging-in-Publication Data

Ross, Nina P.,
     Men of God/ by Nina P. Ross.—1st Ed.
        p.cm.
     Includes bibliographical references and index.
ISBN:0-9668796-9-4   (hardcover)
Missions—India—Men

Printed in the United States of America
1 2 3 4 5 6 7 — 10 09 08 07 06 05

CONTENTS

PREFACE

But seek ye first the kingdom of God, and His
righteousness; and all these things
shall be added unto you.
Matthew 6:33

The books of the Bible were divinely inspired, resulting in a flawless writing of the original manuscripts. Along came translations—The Gutenberg Bible, Martin Luther's translation, the Geneva translation, The King James Bible, and others—all part of man's attempt to air the story of God's creation of the world, God's revelation of Himself to man, and man's redemption through Jesus Christ.

Moses is credited by many scholars with writing the first five books of the Old Testament (the Pentateuch) ca. 1500 B.C. This being the case, he almost certainly would have used ancient documents and oral tradition as the Holy Spirit led him in writing Genesis, since all the events occurred before his time. John wrote Revelation, the last book of the New Testament ca. 90 A.D. It may have taken sixteen hundred years to write the Books of the Bible, but the end result is the greatest of all writings ever undertaken.

Each of the thirty men chosen for study in *Men of God* has a story to tell, a lesson as applicable in today's world as in the world in which he lived. Adam, the first man, was a willing accomplice, plunging the human race into sin. God chose Noah to escape the wickedness of the world, yet his own sons returned to idolatry. Simeon waited for the Messiah and held the Baby in his arms.

Stephen tried to refocus the early Christians from temple religion to belief in Jesus Christ as the coming Messiah. Emphasis is not on man but on God the Father and His work through these men to spread the Word of God to the entire world.

As I passed a crude mud and grass school in India on my way home from a Christian worship service, a young man stepped from the classroom and asked me to come in and teach the fifty young Bible students who were in class. He had been my interpreter when I worked with a women's group the previous year. The teacher had not arrived, and the students were eager for a lively discussion.

How could I refuse an opportunity to share my knowledge, however limited, with these eager young students, whose minds were like sponges, soaking up every bit of information that they could find. They listened intently as I began with "Here am I, send me," and continued through Isaiah's vision and call to serve the Lord. Their ensuing discussion and personal testimonies were an even greater lesson and privilege for me.

Three years later, in 2005, these same students were the target of persecution as they traveled to North India for graduation from Bible College. They were severely beaten, one killed, and several hospitalized in a confrontation with militants as they stepped off the train. Local police did nothing to stop the onslaught which continued for days. The students who were able to attend graduation acclaimed their belief in Jesus Christ as their Lord and Savior even though they had been punished for their beliefs. They received a diploma, a Bible, and a bicycle on which to travel into a village to plant a church in abeyance to God's command to go out into the world and spread the Gospel.

I pray that a study of the Biblical men represented in *Men of God* and the related Scriptures will strengthen the application of the principles of Christianity to your personal life. As you adapt to a changing society, hold on tightly to the unchanging principles of Christianity. To God be the glory. Great things He has done!

Not everyone that saith unto me, Lord, Lord,
shall enter into the kingdom of heaven;
but he that doeth the will of my
Father which is in heaven.
Matthew 7:21

Chapter 1

ADAM

So God created man in His own image....
Genesis 1:27

G od created the heaven and the earth and all that is in it. When He was pleased with each phase of the creation, He created Adam and Eve so that man could have dominion over every living thing. He formed man out of the dust of the ground and breathed the breath of life into his nostrils. Man became a living soul.

God put Adam in the beautiful Garden of Eden, which He had created. Adam would be the caretaker. He had only to tend the garden and eat that which pleased him except for the fruit of the Tree of the Knowledge of Good and Evil. "...for in the day that thou eatest thereof thou shalt surely die."[1] Death would be threefold:spiritual, by the power of sin; physical, as the body begins to decline; and eternal, succeeding physical death (known as second death).

After Adam had given names to all the living creatures that God had created, God caused a deep sleep to fall on Adam. God took one of Adam's ribs and created a woman to be Adam's help meet so that he would no longer be alone. Woman (Eve) was taken from under his arm to be protected by him—not from his head to rule over him, nor from his feet to be stepped on. Thus the two lived, unclothed, but unashamed, in the Garden of Eden, tending the trees and herbs, keeping the roaming animals from destroying its beauty.

Satan appeared to Eve in the form of a serpent. He caused her to doubt God. Eve knew that God had told them not to eat of the fruit of the Tree of the Knowledge of Good and Evil, but He had said nothing about touching the tree. She yielded to temptation without even consulting Adam. As a result of her lust (for food and pleasure)

---

[1] Genesis 3:17

and the desire to become wise, she plunged the human race into sin, sickness, suffering, sorrow, guilt, fear, and death. Adam was her willing accomplice.

Adam and Eve hid themselves as God approached. They were aware of their guilt and were ashamed. Instead of asking God to have mercy on them, they tried to run away from Him. God questioned Adam and Eve, although He was fully aware of their disobedience. He wanted to lay forth their sins before He set their punishment

Adam blamed Eve. Neither accepted the blame. As a result of their disobedience, man was sentenced to a life of sweat and toil and a return to dust at the end of his life. Woman was sentenced to suffering in childbirth. Adam and Eve had two sons, Cain and Abel. Abel was a shepherd, and Cain a farmer. After an altercation, Cain murdered Abel. God gave Adam and Eve another son, Seth, when Adam was 130 years old and other sons and daughters later in his life.

The Creation, as presented in Genesis 1-2, is accepted by many readers of the Scripture as *the way it all began.* The manner of God's creation of man is repeated in Genesis 5:1-5. It is not so important to know how and when God created the heaven and the earth. What really matters is to know the why and the wherefore.

———

Aaron and Evelyn worked hard to provide for their family. The children were well-mannered, as well as well-groomed and caring of others. They attended public schools and were active in Sunday school youth activities.

When their daughter Sonia was twenty-one, she decided to marry Don, a young man from a prominent, well-to-do family. Don did not attend church, never held a job, and felt he was entitled to an easy life.

Sonia pretended she did not know the source of the huge sums of money he often carried around. Her parents were unable to persuade her to date other young men. Their wedding date was set, and Aaron and Evelyn planned a wedding which was well above what they could afford.

The wedding date came, and, when Don failed to show up for the wedding rehearsal, Sonia was devastated. Don had been caught by an undercover agent in a drug deal gone sour. Although Aaron and Evelyn believe that God played a part in the wedding disruption, Sonia feels her life is hopeless.

God forgives our sins, just as He has forgiven Adam and Eve. Yet we must bear the consequences of our sins, just as they have done. They forfeited the right to live in the beauty created for them by God by denying His command. Standing at the foot of the highest mountains makes it easier to comprehend creation and the glory of God.

> *For by Him were all things created, that are in heaven,*
> *and that are in earth, visible and invisible, whether*
> *they be thrones, or dominions, or principalities,*
> *or powers:all things were created by*
> *Him, and for Him.*
> Colossians 1:16

Suggested Scripture Reading

Genesis Chapters 2-5; Deuteronomy 32:8; 1 Chronicles 1:1; Job 31:33; Luke 3:;38; Romans 5:14; 1 Corinthians 15:22, 45; 1 Timothy 2:13-14; Jude 14.

Study Questions

1. God created the heaven and the earth and all that is in it. How would you have felt, being the only human being?

2. God told Adam and Eve not to eat the fruit of the Tree of the Knowledge of Good and Evil. When you are faced with a choice, how do you make a decision?

3. Death to Adam and Eve for disobedience was threefold. What makes death threefold?

4. God caused Adam to fall into a deep sleep. Why was Eve created from one of Adam's ribs?

5. The Garden of Eden was a perfect place. What were Adam and Eve doing there?

6. Satan appeared to Eve in the form of a serpent. Was Eve aware that she was talking to Satan?

7. Eve disobeyed God. What was the result of her disobedience?

8. Adam and Eve hid when God approached. Why?

9. God questioned Adam and Eve. Why did He not just punish them since He already knew what they had done?

10. God forgives our sins. Does that mean we are not held responsible for them?

Chapter 2

NOAH

But Noah found grace in the eyes of the Lord.
Genesis 6:8

God provided a perfect place for Adam and Eve to live—the Garden of Eden. It was rent-free, with the stipulation that they were not to touch the Tree of the Knowledge of Good and Evil. Their disobedience caused physical death to become a reality. Spiritual death occurred the day they sinned.

Just as Adam was created in the likeness of God, his son Seth was born in the image of Adam. Hence were the sons of succeeding generations. Lamech sired a son named Noah, whose name means 'rest'. Each generation turned more and more away from God. Their sins were many. They practiced polygamy which led to a greatly increased population. The men were referred to as giants, not so much as in stature, but in their great strength and the force they used to intimidate others. The hearts of the people were lured to evil. The earth was filled with total violence and corruption.

God was not pleased that mankind, which He had created, was filled with evil. He decided to destroy man, even the beasts were to be destroyed for man's punishment.

But Noah found grace in the eyes of the Lord.[1] He worshiped God and did His will. Three sons, Shem, Ham, and Japhet, were born of Noah. Then God said to Noah, "Make thee an ark of gopher wood,"[2] because God intended to bring a flood upon the earth, a flood to destroy all living creatures.

God made a covenant with Noah, promising to save Noah's wife, their three sons, and his sons' wives. All Noah had to do was to build an ark to the specifications given him by God. Noah was to

---

[1] Genesis 6:8, [2] Genesis 6:14-16

bring two of every living thing—male and female—onto the ark with enough food for all. Noah went to work. He was six hundred years old when he completed the ark.

God gave Noah the signal and Noah began boarding all the creatures onto the ark. Noah built the ark, but God shut and sealed the door. It was seven days from the time Noah entered the ark until the flood began. After seven days, the earth was covered. It poured rain for forty days and forty nights. The flood covered the entire inhabited earth, destroying all living things. It was 150 days from the start of the rain to the time the ark came to rest on Mount Ararat. This was not an ordinary flood from natural causes. This was a flood brought on by the hand and judgment of God.

After 224 days, the mountaintops reappeared and Noah sent out a raven. Seven days later, he sent a dove out of the ark. He again sent a dove seven days later. The final release of a dove occurred after another seven days. Altogether, it was 314 days from the beginning of the launch of the ark until Noah removed its covering. A total of 371 days elapsed from the beginning until the end of the ordeal when Noah was commanded to go out of the ark. God promised Noah that He would never again destroy the entire earth by flood. The rainbow symbolizes God's covenant with Noah.[3]

As part of replenishing the earth, Noah planted a vineyard. When the grapes matured, he made wine. To celebrate, he drank of the wine and became drunk. He lay down naked in a drunken stupor in his tent. His son Ham saw him and reported the incident to Shem and Japheth who covered his nakedness with a garment without seeing his nakedness.

Noah's sons were not satisfied with God's will that they should scatter and replenish the earth. Instead, they built a city and a tower to their own liking. It became known as the Tower of Babylon, Babel meaning 'confusion'. The tower's top was supposed to reach the heavens. It was at this point that the Lord judged them by confounding their language. This event pinpoints the beginning of the many languages found in today's world.

Not only was Noah witness to the building of the Tower, but also to the horrible wickedness of his children, their descent to idolatry, and their bloody, intra-family wars. Noah lived for three hundred fifty years after the flood, making him 950 years old when he died.

---

[3] Genesis 9:8-17

Just as Noah's sons were discontent with God's will, people in today's cultures often experience the same feelings and disbelief. We will never totally understand the will of God. But we must understand that, in God's plan of salvation, we are saved by His grace and not by our own self-effort.

A well-known horse breeder carefully examined all the well-bred racing horses in the country. His goal was to produce an animal so superior in quality that it would win every derby here and abroad. Two-by-two, male and female, he looked at them, felt of them, and studied their pedigrees. When at last he was satisfied that he had the best stud and the best mare, he took them into his breeding stable and ignored all others.

The owners of the rejected horses were indignant. They began to breed their horses indiscriminately until there were more horses than owners to care for them. The horses roamed the land, wild and uncared for. They were so unsightly that they would be hard put to find the gate, let alone win a race.

In the meantime, the mare of the discriminate breeder produced a foal. It was the most beautiful animal ever before seen. As it matured, everyone privileged to lay eyes on it agreed that it could win any race it entered. Two jealous breeders decided to discredit the owner by spreading unfounded claims that the owner used unethical practices in his breeding program. They were not satisfied that the owner was giving them every opportunity to follow his successful methods in producing quality horses.

As a result, horses were scattered throughout the land without identifiable pedigrees. Breeders lost the opportunity to learn from the master breeder, and, in spite of the evil intentions of a jealous few, the young horse, nurtured by a loving master, went on to set an all-time, world horse-racing record.

God chose Noah out of all the people to escape the wickedness of the world. Noah's sons had every opportunity to scatter and replenish the earth. Instead, they followed their own selfish instincts to do as they pleased, returning to idolatry and a quarrelsome atmosphere. God has planted beautiful, sustaining gardens throughout the world. Let us climb aboard His vessel to find peace in His name.

Let the wicked forsake his way, and the unrighteous man his thoughts:
and let him return unto the Lord, and He will have mercy upon him;
and to our God, for He will abundantly pardon.
Isaiah 55:7

Suggested Scripture Reading

Genesis 5 –10; 1 Chronicles 1:4; Isaiah 54:9; Ezekial 14:14, 20;
Hebrews 11:7; 1 Peter 3:20; 2 Peter 2:5.

Study Questions

1. Noah's name means 'rest'. Give reasons parents choose a particular name for their child.

2. The people in Noah's era turned from God. Give reasons God was displeased with them.

3. Noah found grace in the eyes of the Lord. Why?

4. God told Noah to build an ark. What was the purpose of the ark?

5. Noah was in the ark for 371 days. How do you suppose you would have survived that long in the ark?

6. God has given us the sun, moon, and stars, as well as rain and snow. Why did God create the rainbow?

7. After Noah went out of the ark, he planted a vineyard. What do you think you would have done to replenish the earth?

8. Noah used poor judgment in his state of drunkenness. According to Genesis 10:21-27, who was to blame for the outcome?

9. Noah's sons built the Tower of Babel? What was God's will for them?

10. God has provided us with many opportunities to serve Him. What are you doing to magnify God?

Figure 1. Roman Votive Calf.
Bronze calf, 2nd – 4th Century A.D.
The bronze calf, in every size from small to large,
was a votive object in the ancient world, including Egypt.

Chapter 3

ABRAHAM

⸺

I am the God of Abraham....
Matthew 22:32

braham, father of the nation of Israel, is one of the most important men in history. He is first mentioned as Abram, son of Terah. Abram, meaning 'exalted father', and Abraham (to which it was later changed), meaning 'father of a multitude', is mentioned in sixteen books of the Old Testament and eleven books of the New Testament. Judaism, Christianity, and Islam are attributed to him.

Abram and Sarai (later changed to Sarah) were wed. Terah took Abram and Sarai, along with a great grandson, Lot, from Ur of the Chaldees, a pagan center of idolatry, to Canaan. They lived in nearby Haran until Terah's death.

The Lord called Abram to leave Ur for a life of pilgrimage. God's promises included the land of Canaan; a great nation (of Jewish people); great material and spiritual prosperity (for himself and his descendants); making his name known for posterity; and his bloodline becoming a channel of blessing to all the families of the earth.[1]

When the family came to Shechem, Abram built an altar to the Lord amidst the hostility of the Canaanites. Next Abram moved his family between Bethel and Ai. There, too, he built an altar to the Lord. Then he moved southward to the Negev.

Abram had deep faith in his Lord. However, when a famine occurred, he fled to Egypt. He was so concerned that Pharaoh would seize his beautiful wife Sarai and kill him that he convinced her to pretend to be his sister. Actually, she was his half-sister. Sarai had to

---

[1] Genesis 12:3

serve in the Pharaoh's harem. When Sarai exposed the Pharaoh's household to a communal disease, the Pharaoh discovered Abram's deceit and sent the entire family back to Canaan in shame.

Abram's return to Bethel from Egypt was a return to deep fellowship with God. He became an example for those who stray, and "back to Bethel" became their rallying cry.

When the herdsmen of Lot and Abram fought over pastureland for their flocks, Abram gave Lot the choice of the land. Lot chose the lush and fertile Jordan Valley, bordering the sinful cities of Sodom and Gomorrah. Although Lot did not participate in their wickedness, he sat at the gate of Sodom and became a local official.

Even though Abram gave up the choicest pastureland, God gave him and his descendants all the land of Canaan. Abram built his third altar for God in Hebron.

Lot became a captive during a war between the king of Elam and other rebel kings in the Valley of Siddim. When Abram heard the news, he assembled a force of trained men. He defeated them near Damascus and rescued Lot. Upon their return, Abram was met by the king of Sodom. But it was Melchizedek, king of Salem and priest of God most high who offered Abram bread and wine to strengthen him. He blessed Abram, and Abram gave him a tithe of all his captured wealth.

God promised Abram a son. Sarai was past child-bearing age, but Abram believed God's promise. Sarai persuaded Abram to have a child by her handmaid Hagar. Hagar taunted Sarai, who drove her away. The Angel of the Lord counseled Hagar to return and submit to Sarai.

God renewed His covenant with Abram and changed his name to Abraham. God changed Sarai's name to Sarah and promised Abraham that Sarah would bear a son to be named Isaac.

Three men appeared to Abraham. Two were angels and the other was the Lord Himself. Abraham and Sarah showed them great hospitality, unaware of the true identity of their guests. Sarah overheard one of them (the Lord) say that she would bear a child within a year. She laughed and was rebuked with the question, "Is anything too hard for the Lord?"[2]

The Lord revealed to Abraham that He would destroy Sodom. Abraham began an intercessory prayer for the people of Sodom. He went from fifty righteous individuals to forty-five; to forty; thirty; twenty; to ten. And the Lord said He would not destroy Sodom if

---

[2] Genesis 18:14

even ten righteous people could be found. Sodom was eventually destroyed. God remembered Abraham and sent Lot out of the midst of the cataclysm.[3]

When Abraham and Sarah journeyed south and stayed in Gerar, Abraham once again used Sarah to avoid the king's anger. He told Abimelech that Sarah was his sister. The king took Sarah. This time God came to Abimelech in a dream, telling him that Sarah was another man's wife. God worked through the two men, whereby they all were vindicated and Sarah was unblemished.

Isaac was born to Abraham and Sarah a year later as promised. Hagar and her son by Abram (Ishmael) were provided for by God, but God reminded Abraham that Isaac, not Ishmael, was the promised son through whom the covenant would be carried out—a new nation and a deliverer for His people.

The servants of a chieftain in the area confiscated a well of water from Abraham's men. Abraham and the chieftain made a treaty of friendship. When Abraham told him about the seizure of his well, the chieftain made a covenant granting the well to Abraham. Abraham named the well 'Beersheba' (well of the oath). The place later became a city, the southernmost boundary of his land. He planted a tamarisk tree there as a memorial.

God tested Abraham's faith by ordering him to offer up Isaac as a burnt offering in the land of Moriah, a mountain range in Jerusalem (where Calvary stood). "Take now thy son, thine only son Isaac, whom thou lovest...."[4] During Abraham's preparation for the sacrificial act, Isaac asked his father, "Where is the lamb?" To which Abraham replied, "God will provide for Himself the lamb."

As Abraham laid Isaac on the altar, the Angel of the Lord told him to stop. Abraham's fear of God was apparent. Instead of Isaac, he offered up for a burnt offering a ram which was entangled in a nearby thicket. God was pleased and continued to bless Abraham.

Sarah died at the age of 127. Abraham purchased a field with a cave in Hebron to use as her burial place. The cave later became the burial place for Abraham, Isaac, Rebekah, Jacob, and Leah.

Abraham, realizing his old age, called upon his trusted servant to find a wife for Isaac. She must not be a Canaanite or live in Mesopotamia. The servant took ten camels and gifts and went to Mesopotamia to the city of Nahor. It was here at the well that he met Rebekah. Isaac married her and loved her as his only wife.

---

[3] Genesis 19:29, [4] Genesis 22:2

Abraham took a wife named Keturah. They had six sons. He died at the age of 175 and was buried in the cave with Sarah.

⌐══════⌐

We can stretch our muscles, and they are stronger. We can stretch our minds, and we may understand better. But, when we stretch the truth, we shame ourselves.

The king was concerned that many of his servants were telling untruths either to impress him or to hide their wrongdoings. Unbeknownst to the servants, the king cast a spell over his kingdom. Under the spell, whenever someone spoke or acted in deception, that person would lose a tooth. By the same token, when a person did a good deed, a gemlike sparkle appeared in his eyes.

Among the servants were a man and wife who wanted more than anything to have a child of their own. The man had confided in his best friend that he was infertile but not to tell his wife. The wife, thinking how happy her husband would be to have a child, had intimate relations with her husband's best friend. When she became pregnant, her husband was furious, knowing that he had not fathered the baby. He not only wanted to have his wife punished but also to find the man who betrayed him.

The husband took his problem to the king. The king listened politely, then said quietly, "Look for a man with a toothless smile and a sparkle in his eye and you will have your man."

As the husband walked down the lane toward his hut, he noticed that everyone to whom he spoke had missing teeth. He, too, was having more dental problems than usual. Now and then he noticed a sparkle in someone's eyes—the old woman giving a loaf of bread to a beggar; a child guiding a blind man across the road; the old man shooing the taunting children away from the cripple.

As he approached his friend's hut, the husband decided to go in and tell him his troubles. After all, he had already confided in him once. Just as his friend appeared and bade him enter the darkened room, the husband noticed his sparkling eyes and toothless smile. The king's words rang in his ears. "You, of all people!" he cried in disbelief.

Abram used deception when he feared for himself instead of relying on God to guide him through life's tribulations. He learned to trust God totally when God ordered him to offer up Isaac as a burnt offering. He bargained to save Lot from the burning city. And he offered hospitality to the angels of the Lord who said Sarah would bear a child within a year. We are faced with similar choices in our daily lives. When we trust in God, we have the courage to make choices and the confidence to accept God's response. Only then can we look forward with hope, knowing He will give us the strength to bear whatever may come our way. May we pray continually for strength, faith, and trust to sustain us. To God be the glory.

I will say of the Lord, He is my refuge and my fortress:
my God; in Him will I trust.
Psalm 91:2

Suggested Scripture Reading

Genesis 11:26 – Chapter 25.

Study Questions

1. Abraham was first named Abram and his wife Sarah was named Sarai. Why did God change their names?

2. Abraham moved from place to place. What land did God promise to Abraham?

3. Abram built altars to the Lord. Why did he build the altars?

4. Abram used Sarai in acts of deception. Why did he not tell the truth?

5. Abram returned to Bethel from Egypt. What was the meaning of "back to Bethel"?

6. Sarai was barren. What was her reaction to God's promise of a son?

7. God told Abraham that Sodom would be destroyed. Why was Abraham concerned about the people of Sodom?

8. Isaac was born to Sarah and Abraham as promised. Who was Ishmael?

9. One of Abraham's wells was confiscated by another man's servants. Why did Abraham name the well 'Beersheba'?

19. Abraham laid Isaac on the sacrificial altar. What was the greatest significance of this act?

Chapter 4

ISAAC

—◦—

And God said, "Sarah thy wife shall bear thee a son indeed;
and thou shalt call his name Isaac....
Genesis 17:19

G od told Abraham that Sarah would bear a son, even though they were both well up in years, and that his name would be Isaac, meaning 'laughter'. God established a covenant with Isaac.

Isaac was born as God said. Abraham circumcised him at eight days of age. When Isaac came of age, Abraham gave a feast to celebrate his weaning. Sarah saw Ishmael mocking Isaac during the feast. She insisted that Abraham send him and his mother Hagar (Sarah's handmaid) out of the household. Abraham, father of Ishmael, was saddened but did her bidding.

God ordered Abraham to offer up Isaac as a burnt offering in the land of Moriah, a mountain range in Jerusalem where Calvary stood. God had no intention of letting Abraham go through with the sacrifice. He was testing Abraham's faith.

Abraham took Isaac and two young men to the place which God designated. It took them three days to get there. Abraham left the two men and the supplies to go to the exact spot and told them he and Isaac would return after they worshiped. He took Isaac—the burnt offering—wood, fire, and a knife, and went to the spot.

Isaac, seeing the fire and the wood, asked his father where the lamb for a burnt offering was. Abraham answered Isaac, saying, "My son, God will provide Himself a lamb for a burnt offering."[1]

Abraham built an altar and laid the wood on it. He bound Isaac and laid him on top of the wood. He reached for the knife to slay

---

[1] Genesis 22:8

Isaac. At that moment, the Angel of the Lord called from heaven and said, "Lay not thine hand upon the lad."[2] God knew Abraham was sincere in his faith. His faith was the means of his salvation. His obedience to God's instructions was proof of his faith. Abraham saw a ram caught in a nearby thicket. He offered up the ram as a burnt offering instead of his son.

When Abraham decided it was time for Isaac to take a wife, he confided in his oldest and most trusted servant by oath to search for the right person. He stipulated that the wife must not be a Canaanite nor live in Mesopotamia.

Abraham told the servant that the Lord God would send an angel as his guide in choosing a wife for Isaac. The servant carefully prepared for the journey, taking gifts and ten camels. He went to the city of Nahor.

When the servant reached the well in the evening, he made his camels kneel down, knowing the women would be coming to fill their water containers. The servant prayed that God would send the damsel to whom he would say, "Let down thy pitcher, I pray thee, that I may drink."[3] And the damsel would reply, "Drink and I will give thy camels drink also." In this way, the servant would know he had found the right girl.

As the servant was praying, Rebekah came out with her pitcher on her shoulder. She filled her pitcher at the well and was returning to her house when the servant ran to meet her. He said to her, "Let me, I pray thee, drink a little water of thy pitcher."[4]

She not only gave him a drink but also drew enough water to satisfy all his camels. The servant gave her a golden earring and two bracelets, asking who she was and requesting to meet her father that he might spend the night at their house.

As the servant bowed his head to worship the Lord, Rebekah ran to her house to inform them of the meeting at the well. Her brother Laban hurried to the well to meet the servant and take him to the house.

The servant identified himself and presented his request for Rebekah as the bride of Isaac. Laban and Rebekah's father were convinced that the Lord had arranged it all. The servant presented the gifts to the family. They called Rebekah in and asked her if she would go with the servant to become Isaac's wife. She agreed and made preparations to leave the next morning.

---

[2] Genesis 22:12, [3] Genesis 24:14, [4] Genesis 24:17

In the meantime, Isaac had gone out to look over the fields. He saw the camels approaching. When Rebekah saw Isaac, she dismounted from the camel. When she was told that it was Isaac, she covered herself with a veil. The servant told Isaac what had transpired. Isaac married her and had no other wife.

Isaac and Rebekah had been married almost twenty years when Isaac asked the Lord to give them children. Rebekah conceived and was pregnant with twins. She asked God why the twins were seemingly struggling within her. God said to her, "Two nations are in thy womb."[5]

Esau was first-born and Jacob next. Isaac loved Esau and Rebekah loved Jacob. Esau, the hunter, sold his birthright to Jacob, a plain man. However, it was Jacob whom God intended to be the leader of Israel.

A severe famine occurred, causing Isaac to flee with his family to Gerar. God told him not to go to Egypt but to stay temporarily in Gerar. God also reconfirmed His oath to Abraham, "...and in thy seed shall all the nations of the earth be blessed."[6]

Isaac repeated the deceit of his father. He said that Rebekah was his sister because he was afraid he would be killed. When Abimelech found out about the deceit, he reprimanded Isaac who confessed. Abimelech told his people not to harm Isaac and his family. Isaac prospered in the land to the extent that Abimelech asked him to leave. Isaac moved from Gerar to the Valley of Gerar, not far away.

The Philistines had stopped up the water wells which Abraham had dug. Isaac had to re-dig the wells. The Philistines were so unfriendly that Isaac moved away and dug a new well, naming it Rehoboth. From there he went to Beersheba with the Lord's blessing. Isaac built an altar to worship God; pitched his tent; and dug a well. Abimelech and his men caught up with Isaac. Assuring him that they wanted to be friends, they departed in peace.

Approximately thirty-seven years later, Jacob cheated Esau out of the birthright. Isaac was old, feeble, and almost blind. Rebekah plotted the deceit even though God had already promised the blessing to Jacob. Jacob was just as guilty of deceit because he carried out her plans.

As a result of the deceit, Isaac blessed Jacob. When Esau came in from the hunt and found out that Jacob had been blessed through deceit, he begged for his father's blessing, but it could not be retracted.

---

[5]Genesis 25:23, [6]Genesis 26:4

Esau planned to kill Jacob as soon as Isaac died. Rebekah told Jacob to go to Haran to stay with her brother Laban. She told Isaac that she was sending him away so that he would not marry a Hittite. Isaac and Rebekah were grieved over Esau's marriage to two Hittite women. This was yet another indication of his unfitness for the birthright.

Isaac called Jacob to him, blessed him, and sent him to find a wife among Rebekah's people. After many years, Jacob returned to Hebron where Abraham and Isaac had traveled. Isaac was 180 years old when he died. Jacob and Esau buried him in Canaan in the cave alongside Abraham.

Neither Isaac nor his twin brother used good judgment during their relationships with others. God gave them the gift of choice, just as He has blessed us. It is up to us whether our choices become blessings. The wrong choice invariably comes back to haunt us, and, as with sin, we must suffer the consequences.

———

The rich landowner had a large family. He worked hard and expected his children to help in the fields. He was especially fond of Ramu, one of his sons and kept him busy with easier chores close to the house. Ramu had an intolerance of direct sunlight. While the other sons were out chopping weeds, bringing in firewood, and other laborious chores, Ramu sat under the shade of a mulberry tree, whittling or weaving a fishnet.

One day the brothers schemed to get back at Ramu for not having to join them in the fields. They sent one of their sisters who was equally jealous of Ramu to fabricate a story. She told Ramu that their father was really quite ill and needed all the help in the fields that he could get. She said that the brothers knew Ramu could not tolerate the hot sun and that was why their father let him work in the shade of the mulberry tree. She begged him to help their brothers so that they could get their work done faster and spend time with their sick father.

Ramu loved his family and wanted to do everything he could to make them happy. Oblivious to his siblings' treachery, he joined his brothers in the field. His body began to perspire profusely. The more he perspired, the smaller he became. The brothers became alarmed and carried him back to the mulberry tree. By the time they got to the shade, there was nothing left of Ramu but his hands.

Knowing how angry their father would be when he found out their trickery, the brothers decided to bury Ramu's hands and tell their father he had been carried off by bandits.

The loss of his favorite son made the landowner so sad that he began to sit under the mulberry tree where his beloved Ramu used to sit. The only happiness he felt was when he smelled the sweet perfume of a beautiful blossoming tree that appeared, seemingly out of nowhere. Only the brothers knew that the tree grew in exactly the same spot where Ramu's hands were laid to rest.

God has given us the gift of choice. When we make the wrong choice we must pay the consequence. When we choose to deceive, regardless of the person, we ultimately pay for our sin. It is easier to make the right choice when we choose to magnify God in all our actions.

Let us choose to us judgment:
Let us know among ourselves what is good.
Job 34:4

Suggested Scripture Reading

Genesis 17:19-21; Chapters 21-22; 24-28; 31-32; 35; 46; 48-50.

Study Questions

1. Bearing children was rather like a status symbol in biblical times. What are your thoughts on planned-parenthood?

2. God knew Abraham was sincere in his faith. What thoughts were running through Abraham's mind as he prepared the sacrifice?

3. Abraham sent his trusted servant to find a wife for Isaac. Why did he stipulate that the wife must not be a Canaanite nor live in Mesopotamia?

4. The servant reached the well in the evening. How did he know the women would be coming to the well?

5. The servant prayed at the well. What did he ask God as he waited for the women to come?

6. After twenty years of marriage, Rebekah became pregnant with twins. What did God say to her when she asked why they were seemingly struggling within her?

7. Esau was first-born and Jacob next. Which twin did God intend to be the leader of Israel?

8. Isaac repeated his father's deceit when he took his family to Gerar during a famine. What did he do?

9. When Isaac moved to the Valley of Gerar, he had to dig new wells. Why?

10. Isaac died when he was 180 years old. Where was he buried?

Chapter 5

LOT

—————

And there came two angels to Sodom....
Genesis 19:1

Lot was Abram's nephew, his brother's son. When Abram departed from Haran at the command of the Lord, he took his family with him. The entourage included servants and their families, as well as Lot's family. Abram had no children at that time. Others who shared their religion possibly went along as they journeyed into the land of Canaan.

Abram and Lot each had considerable wealth, including flocks, herds, and tents. There was great conflict between the herdsmen of the two; therefore, the two families were unable to stay together on the same land.

Abram wanted to maintain peace between them. He relinquished his own rights and suggested that Lot choose the land where he would dwell. Lot saw that the plain of Jordan was fertile and well watered, so he chose it and journeyed east to live. He pitched his tent toward Sodom. Lot soon discovered how wicked and sinful the men of Sodom were. He did not have the foresight to check out the neighborhood before he made his choice.

Abram stayed in Canaan until the Lord told him to walk the length and breadth of the land for it would belong to him. Abram moved his household to the plain of Manre, which is in Hebron, and built an altar unto the Lord.

Eventually the greed and sinfulness of the kings and peoples of the many kingdoms erupted into war. Lot was taken prisoner with his belongings. When Abram heard that his nephew Lot had been captured, he took his small army of 318 trained servants and pursued the captors. Abram rescued Lot, his family, all their goods, and he made peace with the king of Sodom.

Lot spent much of his time sitting at the gate of the city of Sodom. He was aware of the sinfulness of the people. One evening, two angels approached Lot. He rose to greet them, bowing in respect for them.

Lot begged the two to come to his home for the night, knowing the danger they faced if they stayed on the streets. He would offer them food. They could wash their feet, and have a night's rest before leaving early the next morning to resume their travels. He convinced them to come home with him. He prepared them a meal and baked unleavened bread for them.

Before they could lie down for the night, the evil men of the city encircled Lot's house, demanding to see the two visitors. Lot went out to talk to the men, but he shut the door behind him. The evil men demanded the two visitors, lusting for their handsome bodies. Lot offered them his two virgin daughters instead, a sin overshadowing his kindness to his visitors.

The men were angry with Lot for refusing to let them have at the two visitors. They began to rough him up. The visitors reached through the door and pulled Lot back into the house. They caused the intruders to become blind so that they could no longer see the door or cause trouble.

The angels told Lot to bring his entire family out of the house because they were going to destroy the city and all who were in it. The sons-in-law paid no attention to Lot's warnings. As morning came, the angels said to Lot, "Arise, take thy wife and thy two daughters, which are here; lest thou be consumed in the iniquity of the city."[1]

Lot resisted, but the angels took hold of his hands, the hands of his wife and two daughters, and fled the city. The angels told the family to "look not behind thee, neither stay thou in all the plain; escape to the mountain, lest thou be consume."[2] Lot continued to flee until he came into the city called Zoar.

In the meantime, the Lord destroyed Sodom and Gomorrah, the entire plain, and all the inhabitants. Lot's wife hesitated and looked back at all she was leaving behind. She was turned into a pillar of salt. God remembered Abraham's desire for Lot's safety and sent Lot away from the overthrow of Sodom.

---

[1]Genesis 19:15 [2]Genesis 19:17

Lot and his daughters continued on to Zoar and went to a cave in the mountain. Lot was so sorrowful that his daughters made him drink enough wine to become drunk. They tricked him into committing incest with them. Nine months later, the older daughter gave birth to a son, Moab, and the younger daughter had a son, Ben-Ammi. Here lay the origins of the Moabites and the Ammonites, both sources of evil for Israel. Both daughters basked in their sins.

Rather than facing up to the sinfulness of those around him, Lot chose to look the other way. God does not produce the evil that lurks in the thoughts of all mankind. Yet we pray fervently to Him to overcome evil. Let us pray without ceasing for the strength to withstand temptation.

The manager of the corporate office was a wise man who tried to keep his employees at ease. His directions were simple and easy to follow: Know what your job is and do it to the best of your ability. One of his workers was offended when the manager suggested he try a little harder to fulfill his responsibilities. The worker decided to undermine his superior's authority and, perhaps, cause him to be demoted.

He conspired with two of his co-workers who agreed to go along with his wicked plan in return for favors should he be promoted. The wise manager immediately saw through the plan. He talked with the two would-be accomplices and encouraged them not to abet their friend in his wrongdoing but to teach him to do his job more satisfactorily.

The worker was so set on his evil plan that he refused his friends' suggestions and continued his plot on his own. By this time the entire staff was aware of the situation. The office manager had no choice but to terminate the worker's job. The other workers praised the manager for his tolerance and his willingness to offer help to their friend. They tried even harder to fulfill their job responsibilities. Not only did they please their superior by working more diligently, but also pleased themselves for the positive atmosphere created by their honesty.

Lot was a just man, but he lost everything, including his family, wealth, and his property. It is not enough to be good and gracious. We must have faith in God and follow His will every day if we wish to reap the reward of eternity with Him.

> *And God saw that the wickedness of man was great in the earth,*
> *and that every imagination of the thoughts of his heart was*
> *only evil continually.*
> Genesis 6:5

Suggested Scripture Reading

Genesis 12:4-5; 13:5-14; 14:12-16; 19:1-36;Deuteronomy 2:9, 19; Psalm 83:8; Luke 17:28-9, 32; 2 Peter 2:7.

Study Questions

1. Abram, Lot, and their families went to Canaan. Why did they go?

2. Abram let Lot choose the place where he would settle with his family. Why did the two families not stay together?

3. The people of Sodom were cruel and sinful. What happened to Lot?

4. Lot sat at the gate of the city of Sodom. Who came to him through the gate?

5. Lot was a gracious host. Who came, demanding that the visitors be handed over to them?

6. The two visitors were angels of the Lord. What did they tell Lot?

7. Lot resisted the warnings of the angels. What did the angels do?

8. The angels gave Lot and his family specific directions. What happened to Lot's wife?

9. The Lord had plans for Sodom and Gomorrah. What happened to the cities?

10. The Lord has plans for each of us. Are you following His plan?

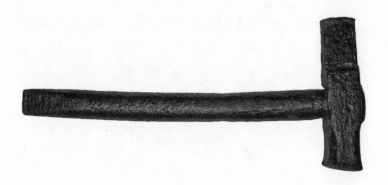

Fig. 2. Roman Hammer.
Made of iron; 3 – 6th Century A.D.
A hammer has not changed much across the centuries.
Solomon was a builder. His men would have used
hundreds of hammers similar to this one.

Chapter 6

ELIEZER

———

And Abram said, Lord God, what wilt thou give me,
seeing I go childless and the steward of
my house is this Eliezer of Damascus?
Genesis 15:2

The name 'Eliezer' appears numerous times in the Old Testament Scripture and again in Luke 3:29. Of the eleven men mentioned as Eliezer, the one to which this writing refers is identified in Genesis 15:2 as Abraham's servant, who would have been his heir in place of a son. Presumably it is this Eliezer who was sent by Abraham to find a wife for Isaac in Genesis 24.

The other men named Eliezer are identified as Moses' second son[1]; a son of Dodavahu who was a prophet[2]; a son of Becher[3]; a priest[4]; a son of Zichri who was a Reubenite chief[5]; a leading man sent by Ezra to find Levites for Temple service[6]; three men who divorced foreign wives[7]; and an ancestor of Jesus.[8]

It was the law during the time of Abram and Sarai, that, since they were childless, their servant, Eliezer of Damascus, would be their heir. God had blessed Abram with wealth because of his loyalty. In addition, God promised him a son, even though he and Sarai were beyond child-bearing years, and changed their names to Abraham and Sarah. God fulfilled his covenant and Sarah bore a son who was named Isaac.

When it was time for Isaac to find a wife, Abraham sent his trusted servant to find the right girl among his own people. She must be of the same religion, race, and social background. She must not be a Canaanite nor live in Mesopotamia.

---

[1]Exodus 18:4, [2]2 Chronicles 20:35, [3]1 Chronicles 7:8, [4]1 Chronicles 15:24, [5]1 Chronicles 27:16, [6]Ezra 8:16, [7]Ezra 10:18, [8]Luke 3:29

The old servant was bound by an oath which involved placing his hand on the thigh of Abraham, his master. Abraham assured the servant that God would send an angel to guide him in choosing the right wife for Isaac.

The servant, Eliezer, accepted the challenge and traveled to Nahor with his ten camels. He knelt by the city well, praying that God would send the girl to the well for water. Then he would say, "Let down thy pitcher, I pray thee, that I might drink."[9] A beautiful young virgin arrived at the well before he finished praying. She gave him a sip of water and offered to draw water—nearly four hundred gallons—for his thirsty camels.

Eliezer was elated that God had led him to the suitable girl. He offered her an earring and bracelets of gold, feeling certain that the young woman was sent by God to be Isaac's bride. He asked permission to go to her house to meet her family. After hearing Eliezer's story, the girl's father and brother were convinced that the Lord had made the arrangements. They consented to the marriage and the young girl—Rebekah—left with Eliezer the next morning to return to Abraham and Isaac. Isaac loved Rebekah throughout their married life.

Marriages are arranged by the parents of the prospective bride and groom in certain countries of the world. Quite often the prospects are still young children. Love is not a consideration. Social class and dowry are determinants.

Eric and Nita lived next door to one another in a middle-class neighborhood. They were in the same grade at school and spent their off-time playing with the other neighborhood children. Their parents, being of differing religious faiths, accepted their children's friendship as a matter of course.

Eric and Nita became teenagers, and their friendship deepened. When Eric invited Nita to their high school prom, her parents reluctantly agreed to the date. However, when the dating continued, the parents became concerned. Their religious beliefs were threatened. Parental disapproval of their deepening relationship only fired their determination to stay together.

---

[9]Genesis 24:14

Eric received a scholarship from a prestigious university in another state. Nita's parents could not afford the high tuition, so she enrolled in a nearby state college. The two exchanged friendship rings as they went off to separate colleges. Their parents were relieved, secretly hoping each would find someone else to love in their new environments.

Although Eric and Nita kept in close touch, they dated others on their respective campuses. They renewed their relationship during semester break with an intimacy that resulted in Nita's pregnancy. She dropped out of school and moved back home. Both sets of parents were devastated. The young couple regretted their indiscretion and considered abortion, which would have compounded their sins, an issue agreed upon by their parents.

Nita has delivered the baby and is living with her parents. Eric continues in his studies, and his parents pay child support. All of them love the child. Nita's chances of finding a new love are minimized—at least until the child is older—and she is on her own again. Eric, on the other hand, continues to date other girls. The couple realized too late that their passion for one another was fueled by their parents' disapproval.

Abraham's servant, Eliezer, was indwelt by the Holy Spirit. The marriage of Isaac and Rebekah, in essence, was arranged by God. God plays a role in finding the right partner. All of us must look to Him, our Lord and Savior, when we are making commitments. Like Eliezer, we too can be indwelt by the Holy Spirit.

> *Then he said, O Lord God of my master Abraham,*
> *please give me success this day, and show*
> *kindness to my master Abraham.*
> Genesis 24:12

Suggested Scripture Reading

Genesis 15:2; Genesis 24.

Study Questions

1. Abraham made a covenant with Eliezer. What was the old servant sent to do?

2. Abram and Sarai were childless. Who would become their heir by law?

3. God had blessed Abram. What were the blessings received by Abram?

4. Abraham assured Eliezer that he would have a guide. Who was to guide him?

5. Eliezer traveled to Nahor. What happened while he prayed at the well?

6. Eliezer liked the girl at the well. What did he do next?

7. Eliezer met the girl's family. How did they react to his story?

8. Marriages are often arranged for children? To whom should young people rely when contemplating marriage?

9. Eliezer was indwelt by the Holy Spirit. What does this mean?

10. Eric and Anita made a mistake. What are the most important things they must do?

Chapter 7

JACOB

⌐⟶⌐

And He said, I am God, the God
of thy father; fear not....
Genesis 46:3

Isaac was forty years old when he took Rebekah as his wife. She was barren for years. He asked God to give them a son. She became pregnant with twins who struggled within her. God told her the twins would represent two distinct nations, one stronger than the other. Isaac was sixty years old when the twins were born.

Esau was born first—thus claiming the birthright—followed by Jacob. Esau grew up as a cunning hunter and Jacob as a plain, indoor type. Isaac loved Esau, but Rebekah loved Jacob. Esau was entitled to twice the portion of his father's wealth, being firstborn. He would become head of the family.

Esau came in from the hunt one day, tired and hungry. He asked Jacob to feed him his favorite food, red *pottage* (stew). Jacob agreed to prepare his dinner in exchange for his birthright. Esau was desperately hungry and swore to Jacob that he would sell him the birthright. After eating the bread and *pottage* prepared for him by Jacob, Esau recovered from his faintness and departed—minus his birthright. Esau preferred physical gratification, while Jacob preferred spiritual blessings.

Rebekah overheard Isaac tell Esau to go hunt for venison. He wanted to taste his favorite meat before he died. Now that he was old, feeble, and almost blind, he knew death was near. Rebekah sent Jacob to bring two young goats, which she would make into Isaac's favorite meal. To further deceive Isaac, she dressed Jacob in some of Esau's clothing. She put the goat skins on his hands and neck. When

Jacob was so dressed and the meat was cooked, he took the bread and stew to Isaac.

Isaac asked who it was that had come unto him. Jacob answered, "I am Esau, thy firstborn…. Arise and eat of my venison, that thy soul may bless me."[1] Isaac was surprised that Esau had found venison so quickly. He wanted to make certain it was Esau by feeling his hairy arms, saying, "The voice is Jacob's voice, but the hands are the hands of Esau."[2] Rebekah's trickery was not necessary. God had already promised Jacob the blessing.[3]

Isaac was totally deceived by Jacob, believing it was Esau whom he blessed. Jacob was just as guilty as Rebekah in deceiving Isaac. Shortly, Esau came in with the venison he had caught and prepared. Isaac trembled in distress when he realized he had been duped by Jacob. Esau begged for the blessing and cried bitterly when Isaac said the blessing would remain with Jacob.

Esau vowed to kill Jacob after their father died. Rebekah heard his words of hatred and decided to send Jacob to stay with her brother Laban in Haran. She told Isaac she was sending him in search of a wife. She did not want him to marry a Hittite as Esau had done. It would be more than twenty years before Jacob returned. Isaac would still be alive but Rebekah would have died.

Isaac told Jacob to go to Padanaram, Rebekah's birthplace, to choose a wife from Laban's daughters. Esau tried to regain Isaac's blessing by marrying a daughter of Ishmael, even though he already had a wife. Jacob left Beersheba and traveled toward Haran to do his father's bidding. He rested for the night on pillows of stones. He dreamed of a ladder reaching from earth to heaven with angels ascending and descending on it.

The Lord stood above the ladder, saying, "I am the Lord God of Abraham thy father and the God of Isaac…."[4] He proceeded to tell Jacob His plans for him. God promised to stay with Jacob. Jacob awakened in fear, feeling the presence of God. He consecrated his stone pillow as a pillar and poured oil on top of it. He named the place Bethel [but the name of that city was first called Luz]. Jacob vowed to follow the will of God. But his faith being weak, he bargained with God, by offering a tenth of all he had *if* God kept His promise.

Jacob continued on his journey to Haran. As he drew near, he came upon three flocks of sheep being watered at a well. He stopped and asked the men tending the sheep if they knew Laban. They did

---

[1]Genesis 27:19, [2]Genesis 27:22, [3]Genesis 25:23, [4]Genesis 28:13

know Laban and said that his daughter Rachel was approaching with Laban's sheep to be watered. When Jacob saw Rachel, he rolled the stone from the mouth of the well and watered the flock. When Jacob told Rachel who he was, she ran to tell her father. They were all happy to have Jacob with them. He stayed a month.

Laban arranged for Jacob to serve him for seven years that he might marry Rachel. On the eve of the wedding feast, Jacob drank much wine. He did not notice that it was Rachel's sister, Leah, who was in the wedding bed until the next morning. Laban had tricked Jacob, saying Leah was older than Rachel and must be wed first. Jacob had to serve another seven years before he could marry Rachel. He loved Rachel more than Leah. Jacob had deceived his father and now he was being deceived by Laban.

Jacob had children through Rachel's handmaid, Bilhah, because Rachel was barren. He also had children by Leah's maid, Zilpah. He had six sons and one daughter by Leah. Then Rachel had a son whom she named Joseph.

Jacob asked Laban to release him from service that he and his wives and family could return home to Canaan. Laban and Jacob worked out a plan whereby all speckled and spotted sheep and goats would belong to Jacob. Laban and Jacob attempted to trick one another by influencing the number of such animals born. In the end, Jacob succeeded in breeding the type animal which would be his. It has not been determined whether this was scientific or miraculous. At any rate, Jacob's wealth increased during his final six years working for Laban.

Laban's sons were jealous of Jacob, saying Jacob had taken that which belonged to their father. The Lord spoke to Jacob, telling him to return to Canaan. Jacob talked to Rachel and Leah, saying it was time to go. He pointed out to them that Laban had cheated him in wages, but God overruled, so that the flocks bred in his favor. His wives agreed to leave secretly with him. Jacob gathered all his belongings, stock, and family. He was unaware that Rachel had stolen her father's idols. They began the journey to Canaan.

Laban discovered the theft of his idols and learned of the family's departure. He and his men set out in pursuit of Jacob. They had traveled for seven days when the Lord came to Laban in a dream, telling him he was not to harm Jacob. When Laban finally caught up with the caravan, he only talked with Jacob, saying he would have given them a decent send-off.

When Laban told Jacob his idols had been stolen, Jacob gave him permission to search the caravan and kill the thief. Jacob did not know it was Rachel who had taken them. Laban did not find the idols in his search. When he came to Rachel's tent, she was sitting on the camel's saddle where she had hidden the idols. She told her father she was having her monthly period and could not rise in the presence of men. Laban searched but did not find the idols.

Jacob was angry with Laban for treating him unfairly for twenty years. After angry words from both, they agreed to make a pact. They were not to harm one another; Jacob was to take no other wives. They marked the pact with a pillar of stones called 'Jegar Schadutha' by Laban and 'Galeed' by Jacob. Neither Jacob nor Laban were to pass the pillar to attack the other. They both swore to uphold the pact. Jacob offered a sacrifice on the mountain, after which they ate and spent the night on the mountain. Early the next morning, Laban kissed Rachel, Leah, and his grandchildren goodbye and left.

On his way back to Canaan, Jacob met a band of angels sent by God. He called the place 'Mahanaim'. He knew he would be passing through the land of Seir in the country of Edom where his brother Esau lived. He was unsure how Esau felt about him after all the years since he cheated him out of his birthright.

Jacob sent messengers ahead to Esau with greetings. The return message was that Esau was coming to meet him with four hundred men. Jacob imagined the worst scenario and prepared his entourage for an onslaught. He prayed desperately for help from his Lord.

That night Jacob was alone after sending his family across the Jabbok (stream). He wrestled all night with the Lord Himself. Jacob's hip was injured and was out of joint. He lost the physical battle, but he won a spiritual victory.

When Jacob admitted who he was, God changed his name to Israel. Jacob named the place Peniel (the face of God) because he realized he had seen God face-to-face, and his life was preserved. He walked with a limp the rest of his life. "Therefore the children of Israel eat not of the sinew which shrank, which is upon the hollow of the thigh, unto this day:because he touched the hollow of Jacob's thigh in the sinew that shrank."[5]

When Jacob saw Esau approaching, he was afraid. He arranged his children with their mothers and handmaids to provide the greatest

---

[5]Genesis 32:32

protection for those dearest to him. After this was done, Jacob went to the front of his entourage and bowed down to Esau seven times.

When they met, Esau greeted Jacob with hugs and kisses. He expressed surprise at seeing Jacob's family. Jacob presented his family and then presented a gift to Esau of three successive *dovers* of animals—580 in all—hoping to appease Esau. Esau at first refused the gift but accepted it after Jacob's insistence.

Jacob refused Esau's offers of help in traveling with the family and livestock to Seir (Edom). He was filled with fear and suspicion at Esau's offer. Instead, Jacob traveled to Shechem where he settled and erected an altar—*El Elohe Israel* (God, the God of Israel).

While Jacob and his family were living in Shechem, his daughter Dinah was sexually assaulted by a son of Hamor. Jacob and his sons refused to allow a marriage between the two. They tricked Shechem into thinking they would agree to the marriage if Hamor, Shechem, and all the other men would be circumcised. The men agreed and were circumcised.(Here the sacred sign of God's law was used in an evil manner.)While the men recovered, two of Jacob's sons murdered them and stole all their worldly goods.

Jacob scolded his sons who retorted that their sister had been treated like a harlot, and they were retaliating. Jacob's real concern was for his own good and not the cruelty rendered to the men of Shechem.

Thirty years had passed since Jacob and Esau had met. God reminded Jacob that he was to go to Bethel and make an altar unto God. Jacob ordered his family to prepare for the journey. Their heathen neighbors were terrified when they saw the family in different dress without the strange gods around them. None of them caused problems for Jacob as he and his household journeyed to Bethel. He built an altar and called the place 'El-bethel' because that was where God appeared to him when he fled from Esau.

God appeared again and told Jacob that he would now be called Israel, saying, "I am God Almighty; be fruitful and multiply; a nation and a company of nations shall be of thee...."[6] Jacob set up a pillar in the place where he talked with God and named it Bethel.

Rachel died in childbirth as they journeyed south from Bethel. She named the child Ben-Oni, but Jacob renamed this, his twelfth son, Benjamin. She was buried on the road from Jerusalem to Bethlehem.

---

[6]Genesis 35:11

Jacob returned to Hebron shortly before his father Isaac died at the age of 180. He dwelt in the land of Canaan. Jacob showed favoritism to his son Joseph, who was sold into slavery by his jealous brothers. They told Jacob that Joseph had been killed.

A great famine occurred. Because there was plenty of food available in Egypt, Jacob sent his ten sons to Egypt to buy corn. Neither Jacob nor his sons knew that Joseph, favored as governor by Pharaoh (King of Egypt) lived there. During the seven years of plenteous crops, Joseph had gathered and stored food so that Egypt had plenty.

Joseph recognized his brothers when they came from Canaan to buy food, but they did not recognize him. He did not reveal his true identity to them. Instead, he played rather clever games with them. They were prepared to offer Joseph a gift sent to him by Jacob (his father) during a banquet Joseph prepared for them.

After a period of time and much *game-playing*, Joseph revealed himself to his brothers. This is one of the most moving scenes in the Bible.[7] Eventually, Jacob and his entire household moved to Egypt. They lived as shepherds in the land of Goshen where they would be isolated from the Egyptians to prevent ill-feelings. Jacob was 130 at this point.

Jacob gained favor with Pharaoh and his household flourished. He had been blessed richly by God, and he wished the same for Joseph. He left Beersheba for Haran when he was seventy-seven. He spent twenty years serving Laban, thirty-three years back in Canaan, and seventeen years in Egypt where he died. As Jacob approached death, he instructed his sons to bury him in the burial place of Abraham and Sarah, Isaac and Rebekah, and Leah. Pharaoh gave Joseph permission to process to Canaan for the burial. The Egyptians mourned Jacob's death for seventy days.

All of us have been richly blessed by God. We do not all use the blessings to return God's love. Those who do are doubly blessed. Those who do not thank God for their blessings and use them to His glory blame everyone but themselves for their tribulations.

The twin boys were very much alike except Ron was larger than Jon. Ron could do everything better than Jon, who was losing his

---

[7]Genesis 45:1-8

self-confidence. If only he could surpass Ron in just one thing—anything—maybe his father would praise him the way he brags on his brother.

The boys were at the swimming pool during summer camp. Ron was showing off his diving skills while Jon played in the shallow end with the other boys who were not strong swimmers. Someone shouted that Ron hit his head on the diving board as he did a back flip. Ron lay motionless on the pool bottom.

Without a moment's hesitation, Jon swam to the spot and did a surface dive. He got a secure grip on his brother's arm and pulled him to the surface. The lifeguard took over at that point. Ron was resuscitated and taken to the emergency room for further treatment and observation.

Jon ran to the dressing room, frantically drying off and dressing. He sat, shivering, waiting for his dad to come for him. What made him, a weak swimmer, think he could save his brother? Where did he get that sudden burst of confidence?

Jacob and Esau were as different as twin brothers could be. Isaac loved Esau more than he loved Jacob. Jacob feared his brother after deceitfully gaining his birthright. Even though God kept his promises to Jacob, Jacob had little faith. As we struggle with problems in our daily lives, we must ask God for guidance, and then have faith that He will lead us. To God be the glory. Great things He has done.

For the good that I would I do not:
but the evil which I would not, that I do.
Romans 7:19

Suggested Scripture Reading

Genesis 25:25-34; 27:6-46; 28:1-20; 29:1-28; 30:1-41; 31:1-54; 32:1-30; 34:1-18;35:1-29; 36:6; 37:1-34; 42:1-36; 45:25-27.

Study Questions

1. Esau was first-born. Why was Jacob entitled to the birthright?

2. Jacob and Esau were not identical twins. Do they share any similarities that would indicate they were twins?

3. Rebekah knew Jacob was promised the birthright. What did she do to show her lack of faith?

4. Rebekah and Isaac sent Jacob in search of a wife. Why?

5. Jacob had a dream while he slept on his way to Haran. What did he learn from his dream?

6. Laban arranged for Jacob to marry Rachel. What happened?

7. Rachel stole her father's idols. How did Jacob respond when Laban told him someone in Jacob's entourage had them?

8. Jacob was unsure how Esau felt about him after all those years. What happened when they met?

9. Jacob's sons killed the men who assaulted their sister. How did Jacob react to his sons' actions?

10. God appeared again to Jacob. Why did He inform Jacob that he would now be called *Israel?*

Fig. 3. Cartonage.
Linen with plaster gesso, painted. Egypt, 600-30 B.C.
Cartonage is the linen and plaster covering
made to protect a mummified body.

Chapter 8

JOSEPH

SON OF JACOB

AND RACHEL

◦———◦

...and the Lord was with Joseph....
Genesis 39:2

Rachel, wife of Jacob, kindled his anger by saying, "Give me children, or else I die."[1] Jacob already had sired children through Rachel's handmaid, Bilhah, and through Leah and her maid, Zilpah. After years of being husband and wife, Rachel and Jacob were granted a son by God. They named him Joseph. It was after this birth that Jacob decided to leave his father-in-law Laban's household and take his family back to his own home. During the ensuing journey, Rachel died while giving birth to her second son whom she named Benoni and Jacob called Benjamin.

Jacob (Israel) loved Joseph more than all of his children. To show his love, he made Joseph a coat of many colors. Sibling rivalry caused Jacob's other sons to hate Joseph.

Joseph dreamed that he and his brothers were binding sheaves, and his sheaf stood in power over theirs. He told them of his dream, and they hated him even more. He told them of his second dream, in which the sun, moon, and eleven stars obeyed him. His father

---

[1]Genesis 30:1

scolded him for upsetting his brothers. Jacob sent Joseph to check on his brothers, who were supposed to be taking care of the sheep in Shechem. A stranger told Joseph that his brothers had gone to Dothan instead.

When the brothers saw Joseph approaching, they decided to kill him and tell their father that a beast killed and ate him. Reuben, one of the brothers, talked them out of it. As an alternative, they stripped Joseph of his coat of many colors and threw him into an empty pit.

A caravan on its way to Egypt was passing. Joseph's brothers pulled him out of the pit and sold him to the passing merchants for twenty pieces of silver. Only Reuben was upset. The brothers killed a young goat and dipped the coat of many colors in its blood. They gave the coat to Jacob who recognized it as Joseph's. He mourned for many days. In the meantime, Joseph was sold in Egypt to Potiphar, one of Pharaoh's officers.

Joseph gained favor in his Egyptian master's house and was given a position of authority. God richly blessed him and those whom he served. However, his master's wife tried to persuade Joseph to have an affair with her. He refused. One day, she caught Joseph by surprise and snatched off his garment. Joseph was so shocked that he ran off.

The wife used the garment to fabricate a story implicating Joseph. Her husband put Joseph in prison. The prison warden favored Joseph and gave him control over the other prisoners.

In the meantime, Pharaoh became angry with his butler and baker and sent them to prison where Joseph was being kept. The two had dreams they did not understand. Joseph interpreted their dreams, one in which the butler was reinstated to Pharaoh's household, but the baker was slain. However, when the butler returned to Pharaoh, he forgot to tell Pharaoh of Joseph's plight. Joseph remained in prison.

Two years later, the butler remembered to tell Pharaoh of the young man in prison who had interpreted their dreams. Pharaoh immediately called Joseph from prison so that he could interpret Pharaoh's dreams.

After hearing of Pharaoh's dream, Joseph said, "God hath shewed Pharaoh what he is about to do."[2] The dream foretold of a great famine and the provisions Pharaoh must make. Pharaoh was so appreciative of Joseph that he made him ruler over all the land of Egypt. Only in the throne was Pharaoh greater than Joseph. During

---

[2]Genesis 41:25

the seven plenteous years and the seven famine years, Joseph married Asenath and had two sons, Manasseh and Ephraim. All the Egyptians and people from other countries came to Joseph's storehouses for food.

Jacob sent his ten sons, Joseph's brothers, to Egypt to buy corn. He was afraid to send the youngest, Benjamin, for fear he would be harmed. Joseph recognized his brothers when they arrived, but they did not know him. They told Joseph that their youngest brother was home with their father. Joseph told the brothers that they would go to prison as spies. One of the brothers was sent to bring Benjamin. Reuben managed to say, "I told you so," in reference to their guilt over selling Joseph into slavery.

Joseph had Simeon bound to remain with him to ensure that his other brothers would return with Benjamin. Joseph filled their sacks with corn as well as the money they paid him and sent them away. The brothers discovered the money and were afraid, saying "What is this that God hath done unto us?"[3]

They told their father, Jacob, all that had transpired when they got home. Jacob refused to let Benjamin go back with them, saying that he had already lost Joseph and Simeon (who was bound and held captive by Pharaoh), and he would not risk losing Benjamin.

The famine continued and Jacob was forced to send his sons, including Benjamin, with gifts and money for more food. When Joseph received them, he had a feast prepared. The next morning Joseph sent them home with great provisions, money, and gifts. He put his own personal silver cup in Benjamin's sack.

Joseph sent his servant after them to accuse them of stealing the money and silver. The servant found Joseph's cup in Benjamin's sack. They were brought back to Joseph who passed judgment on them. One of the brothers, Judah, pleaded with Joseph to let Benjamin return to his father. Joseph could refrain from telling the truth no longer. He burst into tears as he identified himself to his brothers. He asked them to go bring their father, and they would all live nearby in the land of Goshen.

When the brothers returned to their father, Jacob did not believe them until he saw the wagons Joseph had sent to bring him back to Egypt. Pharaoh was pleased and welcomed them.

Jacob and his family lived in the land of Goshen as shepherds, despised by the Egyptians. The famine continued, but by Joseph's

[3]Genesis 42:28

fair and intelligent rule, the people survived. Joseph sold his people seed to sow, with one-fifth of their profit going to Pharaoh.

When Jacob died, the brothers feared that Joseph would seek vengeance on them. Joseph said, "Ye thought evil against me, but God meant it unto good."[4] Joseph died fifty-four years after his father, the first of the twelve brothers to die.

Famines were commonplace not only in the ancient world but also in the present. Newspapers carry heart-wrenching photographs of pot-bellied children, starving to death in Africa and Asia. We have an abundance of food in our country, yet we too are starving. Our famine is lack of love for one another. Neither rain nor financial aid will solve our problem. Only when we obey God's commandment to love Him and one another more than ourselves will we become a well-fed nation.

The poor villagers flocked to their places of worship every morning, bringing with them a portion of their scant provisions to offer to their gods. In return, the priests daubed their foreheads with a sticky, orange substance as a reward for their subservience. Babu had begun feigning illness so that he would not have to go with his family. There was something about the monotonous routine of bowing before a piece of statuary that left him with an uncomfortable, empty feeling.

One morning after his family left for worship, Babu decided to get up and take a walk. He would be back on his pallet beside the hut by the time his family returned. As he walked along the river, he heard music. Curious, he edged closer to the group of villagers sitting under a tree singing. In their midst was a man wearing strange-looking clothing.

When the singing stopped, the man began to speak in a foreign tongue. Another man repeated what he said in a language the villagers could understand. He was saying something about a new way of life. One member of the group recognized Babu and invited him to sit among them. Babu was so engrossed in what the stranger was saying that he barely made it back to his pallet before his family returned.

[4]Genesis 50:20

After several weeks of feigning illness and sneaking away to listen to the stranger, Babu began to change. His father noticed the change and became suspicious. The next morning, instead of going to worship with the rest of his family, the father hid behind a rock just beyond the hut. When Babu came out and headed for the river, his father followed him. He watched Babu join his new circle of friends and kneel in prayer to a new God, one called Jesus. This Jesus was going to give everyone who believed in Him a gift called *eternal life*. Babu must have accepted that gift.

His father, angered by his son's disobedience and saddened by what he must do, trudged back to the hut to await Babu's return. As is the custom, Babu would be punished severely and ex-communicated from his family and village for refusing to worship their chosen gods. With a heavy heart, Babu's father gathered up the family's remaining provisions to be taken to appease their gods.

Many of our co-workers, neighbors, family, and friends are experiencing that same uncomfortable, empty feeling as Babu. If we want God to lead us in our service to Him, we must be willing to follow Him. He does not follow in our footsteps. He has commanded us to go out into the world and spread His Word.

And He answered saying, Thou shalt love the Lord thy God with all thy heart, and with all thy soul, and with all thy strength, and with all thy mind; and thy neighbor as thyself.
Luke 10:27

Suggested Scripture Readings

Genesis 30:22-25; 33:2,7; 35:24; Ch. 37; Ch. 39-48; 49:22-26; Ch. 50.

Study Questions

1. Jacob loved Joseph more than his other children. What usually happens when parents show favoritism toward one or more of their children?

2. Many people dream almost every time they fall asleep. How were Joseph's dreams different?

3. Joseph prospered in his Egyptian master's house. Why was Joseph considered special in his role as slave?

4. The master's wife tempted Joseph. Why did he ignore her advances?

5. Jacob sent his sons to Egypt to buy corn. Why?

6. Egypt had storehouses full of corn during the famine. Why?

7. Jacob had twelve sons. Which ones followed their father's teachings more closely?

8. Joseph recognized his brothers immediately. Why did he not identify himself to them until later?

9. Joseph played games with his brothers before revealing his identity to them. Why?

10. The brothers were afraid Joseph would seek vengeance on them after the death of their father. What other lesson had they failed to learn in all those years?

Chapter 9

MOSES

Let my people go....
Exodus 5:1

Pharaoh issued a decree that said to his people, "Every son that is born ye shall cast into the river, and every daughter ye shall save alive."[1] A baby boy was hidden by his mother until he was three months old in spite of the decree. When she could no longer conceal his existence, she made a basketlike raft for him out of reeds and sealed it with slimy mud. She put the baby into the basket and set it amid the reeds near the edge of the river. His older sister stood at a distance to see what happened to him.

Pharaoh's daughter came to the river to bathe. She saw the basket and told her maid to bring it to her. When she opened the basket, the baby cried. She recognized it as a Hebrew child.

The baby's sister ran over to them and offered to find a Hebrew woman to nurse the baby. She seized upon the opportunity to call her mother to come. Pharaoh's daughter told her to take the baby and care for it. She would pay her for her service.

As the child grew and was weaned, his mother brought him to Pharaoh's daughter to rear. Pharaoh's daughter named the baby Moses because "I drew him out of the water."[2] He lived in Pharaoh's household until he was an adult.

When Moses was forty years old, he found his own people and saw how they were mistreated by the Egyptians. He killed one of them and hid his body. The next day two Hebrews told him he had no right to do that.

Pharaoh found out about it and planned to kill Moses, who fled to Midian. While he sat resting at the well, the priest's seven daughters

[1]Exodus 1:22, [2]Exodus 2:10

came to water their flocks. Having nothing else to do, he helped them. They returned to their father and told him how Moses had helped them. The father invited Moses to stay with them and eventually gave his daughter Zipporah to Moses as a wife. They had a son, whom they named Gershom.

Moses was tending the flock of his father-in-law on the backside of the desert when he came to Horeb (Mount Sinai). The Lord appeared to him in a burning bush. He told Moses to remove his sandals because he was standing on holy ground.(Note:This is the first use of the word 'holy' in Scripture.)During this confrontation, God promised Moses that He would deliver His people from Egypt into Canaan. Moses did not want to face Pharaoh, but God was adamant in His command.

When Moses questioned God, asking Him what he was supposed to tell the people of Israel, God said, "I am that I am.... Tell them that *I am hath* sent me unto you."[3] God knew that Pharaoh would not do as Moses asked until he experienced the divine power, i.e., the plagues God sent on Egypt. The Jewish women were told to ask the Egyptian women for jewelry and clothing as compensation for their bondage.

In his dialog with God, Moses expressed doubt that the people would accept him as God's spokesman. God gave him three signs to convince him of his divine commission. First, his rod, thrown to the ground, became a serpent. When he caught it by the tail, it became his rod again. Next, God told him to put his hand into his bosom. It became leprous. When he put it back into his bosom, the leprosy disappeared. The third miracle involved pouring water from the Nile River onto the dry ground where it became blood.

Moses then complained that he had a problem with public speaking. God responded by saying, "Now therefore go, and I will be with thy mouth, and teach thee what thou shalt say."[4] God became angry with Moses' insecurity and sent his brother Aaron to be his spokesman. Moses was satisfied and returned to Egypt with his family to do God's will.

Moses could not deliver God's message to Pharaoh until he bowed to God's wishes. His wife Zipporah angrily circumcised their son because Moses had neglected to do so, calling Moses *a bloody husband.*[5] Moses sent her and their two sons back to live with her father.

---

[3]Exodus 3:14, [4]Exodus 4:12, [5]Exodus 4:26

Aaron met Moses in the wilderness. They brought all the people of Israel together and Aaron delivered the Lord's message. He gave the three signs which the Lord had given Moses. They all bowed their heads and worshiped the Lord.

Moses and Aaron went to Pharaoh with the Lord's message:Let My people go. Instead of agreeing to let the people go to the feast in the wilderness, Pharaoh heaped more work on them. The Jewish foremen were beaten. When Pharaoh gave them no consolation, they blamed Moses and Aaron. Moses blamed the Lord for the turmoil within the ranks of the Israelites.

The Lord assured Moses that He would keep His covenant with him. Pharaoh would let the Israelites go because God would use a strong hand against Pharaoh. Still, Moses complained of his own speech problems.

The Lord told Moses that he would be as a god to Pharaoh and Aaron would be his prophet. Aaron would convey the messages to Pharaoh, who would not heed, but God would deliver His people anyway. Moses was eighty years old at the time and Aaron was eighty-three.

Aaron confronted Pharaoh a second time, casting down his rod, which became a serpent. Pharaoh's men used magic to cause their rods to become serpents, but Aaron's rod swallowed up their rods. Pharaoh still refused to let the Israelites go.

The Lord caused nine plagues to come upon the Egyptians:the Nile turned to blood; frogs covered the land; dust changed to lice; flies swarmed over Egypt; livestock were killed by pestilence; ashes turned to boils on the people and animals; a hail storm killed men, beasts, and crops; a plague of locust occurred; and there came three days of darkness.

The Lord told Moses that He would bring one more plague upon Pharaoh and Egypt. It would be a plague so severe that Pharaoh not only let the Israelites go, he forced them out. God told Moses to tell the Israelites to ask for gold and silver articles from the Egyptians. At midnight of the appointed date, all the firstborn Egyptians would be slain. Pharaoh heard the warning but still would not let them leave.

Moses and Aaron received detailed instructions from the Lord for preparing the first Passover. It was to be observed by the Israelites on the fourteenth day of their religious calendar as they prepared to travel. Passover meant that the Lord passed over the houses where the blood of the lamb was applied. At midnight, as Pharaoh was fore-warned, all the firstborn Egyptian were slain, and the Israelites were finally permitted to leave Egypt. Approximately two million Israelites left Egypt and began their journeys after spending 430 years in Egypt.

One of the greatest miracles recorded in Scripture occurred when God instructed Moses to lift up his rod and divide the Red Sea. As the sea parted, the Israelites escaped from the Egyptian army which was pursuing them. The sea then closed, cutting off the army.

As Moses led the Israelites on their journey to Sinai, they sang unto the Lord.[6] Their first hindrance was a lack of water during their travel into the wilderness. The Lord came to them and told them to obey Him. He would deliver them from disease and provide for their needs. They found water and palm trees in Elim.

They came to the wilderness of Sin, murmuring against Moses and Aaron because they were tired and hungry. The Lord provided manna, which they gathered and ate according to His orders.[7] At first they did not follow orders and encountered problems. When at last they learned to trust the Lord, they had manna to eat for forty years. The manna stopped when they came to the borders of the land of Canaan.

When they reached Rephidim, there was no water. Again the people rebelled against Moses. The Lord instructed Moses to take elders and go ahead of the people to Horeb. He was to strike the rock that he would find there, using the same rod he used to part the Red Sea. Water flowed from the rock when he did as the Lord com-manded.

Amalek and his army appeared and fought against the Israelites. Moses sent Joshua and his men to fight against him. Moses, Aaron, and Hur went to the top of a hill to watch. When Moses held up his hand, Israel prevailed. When he lowered his hand, Amalek prevailed. Aaron and Hur had to prop Moses' arms up when he became tired so that Joshua's men would prevail. The Lord said He would fight against Amalek from generation to generation. Prayer and the Word of God are the only weapons to defeat evil.

Jethro (Moses' father-in-law) brought Lipporah, Gershom, and Eliezer to Moses for a reunion. Jethro worshiped God. He was sur-prised at the power Moses had over the Israelites and advised him to

---

[6]Exodus 15:1-21, [7]Exodus 16

select men, including rulers, who feared God, were truthful, and did not covet. This would ease the burden of judging the Israelites. Moses took Jethro's advice after which Jethro returned to his own land.

The remainder of Moses' actions takes place at Mount Sinai. The Israelites had been gone from Egypt for three months. The Lord offered the people a conditional law: "If ye will obey my voice indeed, and keep my covenant, then ye shall be a peculiar treasure unto me above all people; …ye shall be unto Me a kingdom of priests and a holy nation."[8] The people were to prepare themselves for what was to come and were ordered not to touch the mount. This was the prelude to the occasion of God's giving the Ten Commandments to Moses on Mount Sinai.[9]

God gave Moses the laws (Ten Commandments).[10] Before Moses left the mountaintop, God told him to summon Aaron, Nadeb, Abihu, and seventy elders. They were to worship away from the Lord, but Moses was to come near Him. When Moses and those he was told to bring ascended Mount Sinai, they saw God in all His glory. After they had eaten, the Lord told Moses to come onto the mount, where He gave him three tablets of stone on which the Commandments were written. Moses remained on the Mount forty days and forty nights.

Moses read the words of the Lord to the people, who said they would obey His command. He built an altar with twelve pillars, representing the twelve tribes of Israel. He took blood from the burnt offerings, sprinkled half of it on the altar and half of it on the people, sealing their agreement to keep God's law.

God proceeded to give Moses instructions for building the tabernacle, setting up the priesthood, and related laws.[11] When Moses finished his work according to God's plans, a cloud covered the tent of the congregation, and the tabernacle was filled with the glory of the Lord. Moses would accompany the Israelites on all their journeys. They moved only when the cloud led them. "For the cloud of the Lord was upon the tabernacle by day, and fire was on it by night, in the sight of all the house of Israel, throughout all their journeys."[12]

Moses' last days are recounted in Deuteronomy 31-34. God still had things for Moses to do, even as his death was imminent, e.g., writing a song for the Israelites. He died at the age of 120 on Mount

---

[8]Exodus 19:5-6, [9]Exodus 20, [10]Exodus 20-23, [11]Exodus 25-40, [12]Exodus 40:38

Nebo in the land of Moab and was buried by the Lord in a secret grave. He was still physically able to lead the people, but he had become spiritually weak. Joshua became his successor.

A scribe asked Jesus which is the first commandment. Jesus answered by saying, "The first of all the commandments is 'Hear, O Israel:the Lord our God is one Lord:And thou shalt love the Lord thy God with all thy heart, and with all thy soul, and with all thy mind, and with all thy strength':this is the first commandment. And the second is… 'Thou shalt love thy neighbor as thyself.'"

The scribe's question was an honest one. His question was straightforward, and he expected a concise statement as an answer. What is man seeking? What is man's purpose in life?Perhaps the following parable illustrates true love as good and evil walk hand in hand.

<hr/>

Once upon a time, in the land of Modos, lived a very wealthy landowner. He had everything money could buy—a spacious mansion, hand-woven Kashmir rugs, the finest dishes and silver. In spite of living in luxury, he was very lonely. His wealth could not buy love. He wanted more than anything to marry a beautiful woman who loved him, not his money. Out of desperation—the years were passing quickly—he went to see the old priest.

The priest listened to his stories of how women wanted his riches, not him. The priest told him that he knew just the right woman. But the landowner would have to be patient and let him— the priest—guide the two in their courtship. The landowner agreed.

Every day for a month the landowner was to have tea with the priest and the woman chosen to be his wife. The landowner came the first day, full of anticipation. The priest and the woman were already seated in the priest's dark study. To add to his dismay, she was clothed in a black cloak-like dress and had a veil covering her head. Only her eyes were visible.

After a month of similar sessions was almost completed, the landowner knew he was deeply in love with this mystery woman. Yet he had never seen her face. The priest told him that tomorrow, their final visit with the priest, the woman would be waiting for him without the cloak and veil. He would recognize her for she would be holding a loaf of bread and a jug of wine for the priest.

The landowner was full of excitement and anticipation as he approached the old priest's humble dwelling the next day. He could barely see the figure of a woman standing by the door. The closer he came, the more troubled he became. There she was, a haggard-looking, unkempt woman—holding a loaf of bread with a jug of wine at her side! His hopes fell. His heart pounded. Is this the woman with whom he had fallen in love? Should he turn and run away?

Remembering the words of the wise, old priest, "Love is from the heart," the wealthy landowner smiled and extended his hand.

"Shall we enter for our usual tea with the priest?" he asked.

"I don't know what you're talking about," the woman replied. "I'm the scrubwoman here. All I know is that a beautiful young woman handed me this loaf and wine as she went in to see the priest. She said, 'Hand it to him if he chooses to come in.'"

God is at the top of the list in man's life with no other love to rival love for God. In addition we are to love our neighbors. We are to love God more than ourselves and our neighbors as ourselves.

God is just as concerned with what we are inwardly as what we are outwardly. He sees what is in our hearts. We cannot deceive Him with external religion, by participating in religious ceremonies and putting on public displays of our piety. We must have inward, personal holiness. We must ask God to cleanse us from sin and give us the strength to live as He would have us live.

That thou mayest love the Lord thy God,
and that thou mayest obey his voice, and that thou mayest cleave unto
him: for he is thy life, and the length of thy days: that thou mayest
dwell in the land which the Lord swore unto thy fathers,
to Abraham, to Isaac, and to Jacob, to give them.
Deuteronomy 30:20

Suggested Scripture Readings

The Pentateuch; Matthew 17:3; 23:2; Luke 9:30; John 9:28; Hebrews 10:28.

Study Questions

1. Pharaoh decreed that all baby boys were to be cast into the river. Why was Moses allowed to live?

2. Moses lived in Pharaoh's household. How did he learn of the plight of the Hebrew people?

3. Moses was tending his father-in-law's flock in the desert. Why did God confront him?

4. Moses complained of speech difficulties and God involved Aaron in negotiations with Pharaoh. What implications does the involvement of Moses' family in his life have for families in today's society?

5. Moses expressed doubt that the people of Israel would accept him as God's spokesman. How did God convince him of his divine commission?

6. Zipporah became angry with Moses. Why?

7. Moses and Aaron took the Lord's message to Pharaoh. What was the Lord's message?

8. The Lord sent plagues to convince Pharaoh to bow down. What were the plagues and what effect did they have on Pharaoh?

9. God gave Moses and Aaron detailed instructions for the first Passover. What was the first Passover?

10. There are many great miracles recorded in Scripture. Why were the Israelites able to escape from the Egyptian army?

Fig. 4. Two-handled Decanter.
Ca. 1500 B.C. Similar to vessels used during the time of Abraham.

Chapter 10

AARON

For they cast down every man his rod, and they became
serpents:but Aaron's rod swallowed up their rods.
Exodus 7:12

Aaron, whose name means 'enlightened, rich mountaineer', was the son of Amram and Jochebed. He had an older sister, Miriam, and a younger brother, Moses. Aaron is not mentioned in the rescue of baby Moses from the river. It is Miriam who intercedes for her mother and saves Moses from death by Pharaoh and from perishing in the river. Aaron married Elisheba, who was the daughter of a prince of Judah. They had four sons, Nadab, Abihu, Eleazar, and Ithamar. Nadab and Abihu were destroyed by fire from the Lord for offering Him *strange fire*.

Aaron was eighty-three and Moses eighty when God made Aaron Moses' spokesman in their encounters with Pharaoh. Aaron was superior to Moses in oratorical ability. Moses would receive God's instructions on how to deal with Pharaoh, and Aaron would announce God's plans to the people. The preceding chapter on Moses gives insight into their work together to free the Israelites from Pharaoh's control in Egypt. Aaron and Moses worked and worshiped together as a team.

Aaron became the first high priest of Israel. He was appointed to the priesthood by Moses. He may have had strong oratorical skills, but he was weak in character. He incurred Moses' wrath by giving in to the people when they demanded a golden calf. He participated with them in idolatry. Miriam talked Aaron into *murmuring* against Moses. He joined her in jealous criticism of Moses. As a result,

Miriam was smitten with leprosy. Aaron was spared because of his priestly status. Together he and Moses prayed for Miriam's recovery.

Neither Aaron nor Moses was allowed to enter the Promised Land. They had taken the credit for what God had done through them instead of magnifying God. Aaron died on Mount Hoc at the age of 123. His son Eleazar succeeded him in the priesthood.

Moses and Aaron lived over 3,000 years ago. Yet they are thought of as role models today, epitomizing the necessity of joining together as a team in God's work. We too must join with others, working together as God uses us to do His will. God is in control.

———

Ed and Robert started kindergarten together. By the time they were in high school, they were inseparable. Ed was good in sports and spent hours in the exercise room at the gym. He passed all his courses, although his grade point average was below average. Robert, on the other hand, excelled in school and was awarded a scholarship to a prestigious university. Despite their differences, the two remained friends.

Ed tried playing sports professionally but did not quite measure up. He went from job to job, never really satisfied with his work. He married a girl from out of town. She tired of his inability to stick with a job and divorced him. One day he received a call from a former coach who always felt Ed had the potential to succeed. The coach had heard that a sporting goods company was interested in opening a retail store and was looking for a management trainee. Was Ed interested?

Robert, in the meantime, had earned his master's degree in business management and had formed his own business conglomerate. He and his young family were happily situated in a neighboring city. They were active in civic affairs and in their local church. Even though Robert had heard that his long-time friend was struggling, he was surprised when he received a telephone call from Ed. Before the conversation had gone far, Robert knew that Ed was going to ask for financial aid. As he listened to Ed, he was formulating his answer.

Aaron and Moses were brothers, yet they were different. Aaron had a weak character. He gossiped about his own brother. He was jealous of his brother's relationship with God. Aaron did have strengths, and God used those strengths to supplement Moses' weaknesses. They worked together as a team. They were successful because they moved forward together.

Robert found himself in much the same situation with Ed. Ed had his weaknesses, but he was successful as a team member in sports. Would he be able to transfer that skill to a business situation? Robert would turn to God in prayer before he gave Ed a *yes or no* answer. God was on his team.

Behold, how good and how pleasant it is for brethren to dwell together in unity. It is like the precious ointment upon the head, that ran down upon the beard, even Aaron's beard; that went down to the skirts of his garments.
Psalm 133:1-2

Suggested Scripture Readings

Exodus – Numbers; 1 Chronicles 6:49; Psalm 105, 133:1-2; Luke 1:5; Acts 7:40; Hebrews 5:4, 7:11, 9:4.

Study Questions

1. God became angry with Moses. How had Moses failed God?

2. Moses had a weakness. What did God tell Aaron to do?

3. God gave Moses and Aaron the wherewithal to perform three miracles. What was to happen when Aaron and Moses cast their rod before Pharaoh?

4. Pharaoh's men repeated Aaron and Moses' act. Why were Pharaoh's men able to mimic the miracle?

5. The Lord gave Aaron miracles to use against Pharaoh. What was the purpose of the miracles?

6. Aaron was a priest. Who appointed him to the priesthood?

7. Aaron and Miriam were siblings of Moses. Why were they jealous of him?

8. Aaron and Miriam disobeyed the Lord. What did they do to cause God to become angry with them?

9. Miriam was smitten with leprosy because of her disobedience. Why was Aaron spared?

10. Aaron and Moses used all the weapons given to them by the Lord. Why were the Israelites able finally to leave Egypt?

Chapter 11

BOAZ

*And Naomi had a kinsman of her husband's, a mighty man
of wealth, of the family of Elimelech;
and his name was Boaz.*
Ruth 2:1

Boaz was a mighty man of wealth from the family of Elimelech.
His father was Salma (or Salmon). In building the house of
the Lord at Jerusalem in Mount Moriah, Solomon followed
the Lord's instructions. When he erected the pillars in front of the
Temple, he called the pillar on the right Jachin and the one on the
left Boaz.

Boaz returned from Bethlehem and went to check on the reapers
working in his fields. The law provided that the Israelites must leave
some grain in the fields when harvesting to provide for the needy. He
asked the identity of the young woman who was in the field. The
reapers explained that she was the woman who had come back from
Moab with Naomi after the death of Elimelech, Naomi's husband. Her
name was Ruth. Boaz was a close relative of Elimelech. Ruth was married to Mahlon, a son of Elimelech. Mahlon died ten years later.

Ruth stayed longer after working in the field than the others.
Boaz invited her to stay there with his maidens. She could eat and
drink at will, and the men in the fields were ordered not to bother
her. Ruth thanked him and coyly asked why she had found favor
with him. Boaz told her that he was impressed by her actions in
respect to being widowed, yet taking care of Naomi in a strange land.

Boaz praised Ruth for being loyal to Naomi. He offered a little
prayer for her: "The Lord recompense thy work and a full reward be

given thee of the Lord God of Israel, under whose wings thou art come to trust."[1]

Boaz ordered his men to make sure Ruth had plenty of barley to take back to Naomi. Naomi was impressed and asked where she had gleaned the barley. Ruth told Naomi about Boaz, saying he was kin to them. She worked there until the end of the harvest.

Naomi coached Ruth to get cleaned up and make herself appear more attractive. She was to lie down in Boaz's sleeping space, and, when he discovered that she was there, he would tell her what to do. She followed Naomi's instructions.

At midnight after Boaz had eaten and drunk, he lay down at the end of the heap of corn. He was startled when he discovered Ruth's presence. She identified herself, and they discussed the possibility of his marrying her. He could not marry her if the next kinsman in line did his duty and married her. Boaz gave her plenty of barley and sent her back to Naomi.

Under the Law of Moses, when a man died childless, a close relative should marry the widow. In this way, not only was the family name perpetuated, but also the land was kept in the family. Naomi was pleased, saying that Boaz would not rest until the matter of who would marry Ruth was settled.

The next morning Boaz went to the gate of the city, where he found the next of kin. They sat down to talk after Boaz rounded up ten elders. Boaz then explained that Naomi had come back from Moab where she had sold a parcel of land belonging to their brother Elimelech (her late husband). He suggested that his kinsman redeem the property to keep it in the family, but the kinsman declined. His reasoning was that it would complicate his own inheritance. He gave Boaz the right to purchase the property, pulling off his shoe and giving it to Boaz. This was a testimony of Israel. Boaz pointed out to all the people that they were witnesses to the fact that he had redeemed all of Elimelech's property. In addition, he was entitled to Ruth. They all said, "We are witnesses."

Boaz took Ruth as his wife. They had a son whom Naomi nursed as her own. The neighbors named him Obed. He later became the father of Jesse, the father of David. Boaz, whose name means 'fleetness strength', exemplifies a concerned relative. He bought back the land that had belonged to Elimelech to continue the family name.

---

[1]Ruth 2:12

The young woman trudged along the dusty pathway. The noonday sun glared down on her as if reprimanding her for spoiling the barren landscape with her very presence. She came to the well for water when no one else was there. Even her own family had disowned her. All because she had followed her heart instead of her head. The baby, born out of wedlock, died shortly after birth. The man who had promised her the world married someone else. She was confused. Her love had been sinful. Now she was paying the consequences of her sin. She lifted the overflowing water jug to her head, feeling the coolness of the water as it ran down her face, diluting her salty tears so that they no longer burned her eyes.

As she retraced her steps down the dusty road, a shadow appeared from nowhere. Then the robed figure of an old priest stood in her way. Her first impulse was to ignore him and to keep on walking. It was old Pagi. He had lost favor with the elders for befriending her. "God's first commandment is to love Him with all your heart," he had told her. "His second commandment is to love your neighbor as yourself."

"And what about the third commandment," she wanted to blurt out, the one her family and friends used in condemnation of her unfortunate love of a man who was promised to her, yet had deserted her.

"Set down your jug of water and rest yourself here on the rock," said old Pagi. "Your jug of water will not quench your thirst. You must drink of the Lord. Then you shall never thirst."

God works through believers like Boaz and Pagi to give new direction to those wandering aimlessly on the dusty path. Boaz emulates many of the characteristics we envision in a Christ-like figure. He was compassionate. He was aware of Ruth's situation. He used his wealth to help those in need. And he granted Ruth protection and prosperity for her future. Are not these things offered to us through Christ?Just as Ruth stayed in Boaz's fields, neither should we wander from the Lord's promise for life eternal. We must wait patiently and pray without ceasing as God's will is done.

The Lord recompense thy work, and a full reward
be given thee of the Lord God of Israel, under
whose wings thou art come to trust.
Ruth 2:12

Suggested Scripture Readings

Ruth 2, 3, 4; 1 Chronicles 2:11-12; 2 Chronicles 3:17; 1 Kings 7:21.

Study Questions

1. When Solomon built the Temple, he named the left pillar Boaz. Why did Solomon name the pillar to honor Boaz?

2. Boaz saw a strange, young woman working in his fields. Why was he interested in her in particular?

3. Boaz was told that Ruth had returned from Moab with Naomi. Why was Boaz eager to find Elimelech's nearest of kin?

4. Naomi coached Ruth to further her relationship with Boaz. In reality, whose plan did Naomi feel was coming to pass?

5. The Law of Moses came into play here. How did the law provide for childless widows?

6. Boaz and the eligible kin met at the city gate. Why did he take off his shoe?

7. Boaz and Ruth had a son. Why did Naomi rear the child?

8. The story of Ruth and Boaz is a love story. What are some of the lessons to be learned from their story?

9. Boaz had Christ-like characteristics. What was he like?

10. We often become over-involved in earthly activities. What is the Lord's promise to us?

Chapter 12

ELI

Then Eli answered and said, "Go in peace:
and the God of Israel grant thee thy petition
that thou hast asked of Him."
1 Samuel 1:17

E li was a high priest of Israel at Shiloh. He was sitting in the Temple when Hannah, one of the two wives of Elkanah, came into the Temple. She was bitter because she had no children. She wept and vowed to the Lord that if He gave her a son, she would give the son back to Him.

Eli thought she was drunk because no sound came out of her mouth even though her lips moved. Eli told her to stop drinking. Hannah told him her story. After hearing her tell of Elkanah's children by his other wife, Eli told her to stop weeping for God would grant her a child.

Hannah conceived and gave birth to a son whom she named Samuel, meaning 'asked of God'. When the child was weaned, Hannah and Elkanah took him to the Temple and left him in the custody of Eli "for as long as he liveth he shall be lent to the Lord."

Eli had two sons who did not know the Lord. They robbed people and did not follow the law in regard to the preparation of the sacrificial meat. They took meat before the fat had been offered to God. They preferred to roast their meat instead of boiling it.

Samuel was growing up with the two boys, but he did exactly as he was instructed by Eli instead of giving in to peer pressure. He was a devoted child, eager to learn and to serve his Lord. His parents visited him once a year, bringing garments Hannah had made for him.

After Samuel's birth, Hannah gave birth to three more sons and two daughters.

When Eli was very old, he heard about the evilness of his sons. He confronted them and told them to act differently. His reproof lacked sternness, and they ignored his words. Samuel, however, continued to grow in favor with the Lord and with the people of Israel.

A man of God appeared unto Eli. He condemned Eli for allowing the wickedness of his sons and letting it take priority over God's will. He announced the end of the priestly line of Eli and his sons. He told Eli that, because of his wickedness, his two sons (Hophni and Phinehas) would die on the same day, thus ending the priesthood in that lineage. A new faithful priest, Zadok, was promised.

Eli grew weaker and was almost blind. During the time Samuel was serving the Lord at Shiloh, the Lord seldom spoke in visions to men. When Samuel heard a voice calling to him in the night, he thought it was Eli. He ran to Eli, who told Samuel he had not called. The same thing happened two more times. Eli realized that it was the Lord calling Samuel. He told Samuel that if it happens again, he should say, "Speak, Lord; for thy servant heareth."

When the Lord called the fourth time, Samuel answered, "Speak; for thy servant heareth." The Lord confirmed to Samuel His judgment against Eli and his family. Eli was just as guilty as his wicked sons because he did nothing to restrain their evilness.

Samuel was hesitant to tell Eli, but Eli called to him and asked to hear all the things the Lord told Samuel. The word soon became known throughout Israel that Samuel was established to be a prophet of the Lord.

During a bitter war in which the Israelites were losing, they had the Ark of the Covenant of the Lord brought from Shiloh into their camp. They thought that having the Ark with them would turn the battle to their favor. However, thirty thousand soldiers were killed. Eli's two sons, Hophni and Phinehas were killed. And to compound matters, the Ark was captured.

When the news was delivered to Eli, he fell off his seat, broke his neck, and died. He was ninety-eight at the time. Phinehas' wife was pregnant. When she heard the news, she went into labor and died.

Child-rearing practices have changed with time. Proverbs 13:24 admonishes parents with "He who spares his rod hates his son. But he who loves him disciplines him promptly," while modern day child psychologists strongly suggest that paddling children who misbehave promotes deep psychological problems. The following parable holds a different premise.

The strict father beat his three sons unmercifully when they disobeyed him. In his own way, the father loved his children. He was rearing them in the same way he had been reared:Spare the rod and spoil the child. The children, in return, showed proper respect—not love—for their father.

The oldest son, on his eighteenth birthday, knocked his father to the floor, saying, "You'll never beat me again, old man," and walked out of the house. The middle son made it a point to be so involved in extra-curricular activities that he was seldom home when his father was there. The father, however, continued to whip him whenever their paths crossed.

The youngest son, observing what worked and what did not work for his two brothers, developed a totally different strategy. He did little things to comfort his father, bringing his slippers, handing him the daily newspaper, bringing him a cup of coffee, doing his chores without being told—the list was endless. While the whippings continued, they were less severe.

The oldest son eventually married and had children. He found himself following in his father's tradition by paddling his children for the least offense. The middle son married after he graduated from college. He found himself so involved in community activities that he was seldom home. Rearing of the children was left up to his wife.

The youngest son studied to become a teacher and was hired to teach in an elementary school. He treated his students with the same respect that he treated his own children. If they made a mistake in judgment, he talked it over with them, pointing out what was right and what was wrong. He assured them that they would be punished if they deliberately repeated the same mistake. Punishments usually consisted of time-out, loss of privileges, or extra chores/homework.

All three young fathers loved their children. Their own father greatly influenced their parenting skills.

Eli was lax in disciplining his sons. He not only lost their love and respect, but also lost his priesthood, their lives, and his lineage.

Discipline meted out by parents is not perfect. Although it may seem best to them—according to what they think is correct and according to the way they were disciplined as children—it may not always be correct. No discipline seems pleasant at the time. God disciplines us so that we may share in His holiness. The absence of spiritual discipline weakens the core of life.

> *Now no chastening seems to be joyful for the present,*
> *but painful; nevertheless, afterward it yields*
> *the peaceable fruit of righteousness to*
> *those who have been trained by it.*
> Hebrews 12:11

Suggested Scripture Readings

1 Samuel 1-4; 14:3; 1 Kings 2:27.

Study Questions

1. Eli was in the Temple when Hannah came. Why did he think she was drunk?

2. Hanna conceived. Why did she name her son Samuel?

3. Hannah took Samuel to live with Eli in the Temple after he was weaned. Why?

4. Eli had two sons of his own. How did they behave?

5. Eli told his sons to behave. What kind of parent was Eli?

6. A man of God appeared to Eli. Why did he condemn Eli?

7. Eli was a high priest at Shiloh. What did the man of God tell Eli?

8. Samuel heard a voice calling him at night. Why did he think it was Eli?

9. The voice called four times. How did Samuel answer?

10. The Israelites were losing a bitter war. Why did they bring the Ark of the Covenant into their camp?

11. Having the Ark did not turn the tide of the war. What do we sometimes do to try to have things our own way?

12. Eli heard the news of the war. What happened to Eli?

Chapter 13

SAMUEL

⟜——⟜

Wherefore it came to pass, when the time was come about
after Hannah had conceived, that she bare a son,
and called his name Samuel, saying, Because
I have asked him of the Lord.
1 Samuel 1:20

The two Old Testament books of Samuel span the interval between the judges and the establishment of the royal line of David. They become a timeline of God's dealings with Israel from the twelfth to the early tenth century B.C., portraying Samuel, the prophet-judge; Saul, the rejected king; and David, the shepherd king. Samuel's life and deeds, as well as the history of Israel throughout the reign of Solomon and David, are tabulated.

Elkanah, a Levite from Ramathaim Zophim in Ephraim, had two wives, Hannah and Peninnah. Even though Hannah was childless, Elkanah loved her more. She was taunted by Peninnah until she could stand it no longer. On one of their annual visits to the Temple in Shiloh, Hannah vowed to God that if He would give her a son she would give him back to the Lord.

Eli, the old priest, watched as Hannah pleaded with God, thinking she was drunk. After he listened to her story, he told her she would have a son. She kept her vow when the baby was born, naming him Samuel (asked of God). When Samuel was weaned, Hannah took him to the Temple, where he grew up, assisting Eli and the priests and ministering before the Lord.

Chapter 2:1-10 is known as Hannah's Song in which she pours out her heart in thanksgiving to God. Eli's sons were wicked, robbing people and shirking the law. Samuel remained devout in his relationship with the Lord, not bowing down to peer pressure from the sons. When Eli finally woke up to the evilness of his sons, it was too late to do anything about it. He scolded them, but his scolding had no effect. God rebuked Eli for allowing his sons to grow up as evil-doers. The family lineage of priests would end with Eli. His sons would die, and the wife of Phinehas would die in childbirth.

During the time Samuel was growing up in the Temple at Shiloh, the Lord seldom spoke in visions among men. One night Samuel heard a voice calling him. He thought it was Eli. When he checked on Eli, it was not he who called. It happened two more times. Eli advised Samuel to answer the next time by saying, "Speak, Lord, for Thy servant heareth." When the Lord called the fourth time, Samuel answered Him. The Lord confirmed the judgment against Eli and his house, with two witnesses—the man of God[1] and Samuel.[2] At first, Samuel was afraid to tell Eli what the Lord said, but he eventually gave him the entire message.

The Israelites were losing a battle with the Philistines. They brought the Ark of the Covenant of the Lord onto the battlefield to bolster the morale of their army. Nevertheless, they were defeated, and the Ark, too, was captured. Eli's sons were killed. Upon hearing the news, Eli fell backward and died. Phinehas' wife went into labor and died. As she died, she named her newborn son Ichabod.

The Ark was brought to the house of Abinadab in Keyath Jearim where it was kept for the next twenty years. Samuel urged the people to give up their idols and return to the Lord. They repented. The Philistines attacked during Mizpah. Samuel offered a burnt offering, and God turned the enemy away. Samuel set up a stone monument in gratitude, calling it Ebenezer (stone of help).

Samuel's own two sons were wicked. He did nothing to correct them. Like Eli's house, Samuel's house was rejected. The elders refused his sons. They wanted a king like the other nations. The Lord told Samuel to go along with their wishes, but to forewarn them that the king would use the people to enrich himself at their expense.

Saul and his servant were looking for his father's donkeys. They went to a nearby city to ask a man of God about the whereabouts of the animals. A group of women told them that the *seer* (Samuel) would be attending a religious festival there. The Lord would direct Samuel to the man. When they met, Samuel told Saul that the donkeys were being cared for and that Samuel would talk with him in the morning.

---

[1] 1 Samuel 2:27, [2] 1 Samuel 3:14

Saul was given a place of honor at the banquet that evening. The next morning as Saul was departing, Samuel revealed the word of God to him—that he would be king.

Samuel anointed Saul as ruler of Israel. The Lord gave three signs to confirm His word: Two men would meet him at Rachel's tomb, telling him that his father's donkeys were found; three men would meet him at Tabor with two loaves of bread; and he would meet a group of prophets at the hill of God, where the Spirit of the Lord would come upon him, and he would prophesy. All these signs occurred.

Samuel assembled the people to tell them of their new king, reminding them that it was against God's will. The next days were tumultuous, with the people imploring Samuel to help them. If they would obey God, He would bless them. If not, He would bring His wrath down upon them.

Saul disobeyed God and was taken from power. Samuel regretted for the rest of his life that he had made Saul king. God sent Samuel to find the next king, a son of Jesse—a young man named David. Samuel secretly anointed him, but it was years before it became known. Saul was unaware that David bore the Spirit of the Lord. Saul grew fond of David and made him his armor-bearer.

Samuel died and was buried in his house at Ramah. All the Israelites mourned his death.

Samuel, like Eli, was a godly man. He and Eli both served their Lord with good intentions. Yet they disobeyed God, and their people, including their sons, went astray. The following parable illustrates the demise of hungry sheep when their good shepherd becomes side-tracked.

Hundreds of parishioners crowded into the beautiful new sanctuary Sunday after Sunday to worship God and listen to the sermon based on the Holy Scripture. It was soon necessary to schedule an additional service tailored to meet the needs of the spiritually immature people who responded positively to a more contemporary service.

Attendance at the traditional service began to taper. Various efforts to revitalize the service were ineffective. Many long-time members, like hungry sheep, roamed the city, looking for spiritual nourishment.

Contented sheep, roaming the rolling hills in ancient Israel, looked much like fluffy white clouds from a distance. Unlike the dark storms brewing among a people who had turned their backs on God, the sheep were satisfied. They multiplied greatly under the care of a loving shepherd who fed and tended them as God had commanded.

Stray sheep, searching for food, dotted the sun-burned landscape. Their grayish, unkempt, woolly coats were indicative of the tumult permeating the idol-worshiping people who had turned to the paganism of their self-serving rulers. There was no one to feed the sheep, and they were left to struggle for their very existence.

The kind and gentle shepherd, filled with compassion, left his flourishing flock unattended for days on end while he rounded up the strays. A few of his more adventurous lambs joined him, some out of curiosity, while others were ready for a challenge. A new flock was formed, and it thrived under the care of the shepherd.

The shepherd spent much of his time with the new flock. Many of the sheep in his old flock died from malnutrition, and some just wandered away. Others sought a new shepherd. No new lambs were born into the fold to increase its numbers. The once well-fed flock was destined for extinction.

Spiritual hunger is a form of malnutrition. Eli and Samuel each let their sons die of spiritual hunger. Their people strayed from doing God's will. The same thing is happening today in all parts of the world. Are you a sheep or a shepherd?

And I will gather the remnant of my flock out of all countries
whither I have driven them, and will bring them again
to their folds; and they shall be fruitful and increase.
Jeremiah 23:3

Suggested Scripture Readings

1 Samuel 1-4; 7-13; 15-16; 19; 25:1.

Study Questions

1. Eli told Hannah she would bear a son. Why did she name her son Samuel?

2. Samuel grew up in the Temple with Eli's two sons. Why was Samuel not like Eli's sons?

3. Eli heard about the evilness of his sons. How did God rebuke Eli?

4. Samuel thought he heard Eli calling him during the night. What was really happening?

5. The Lord spoke to Samuel. What did the Lord tell Samuel?

6. The Israelites were being attacked by the Philistines. What did the Israelites do to bring themselves luck?

7. God turned the enemy away. What did Samuel do to magnify God?

8. Samuel's own two sons were wicked. What was God's punishment to the house of Samuel?

9. The Israelites wanted to be ruled by a king like the other countries. How did God react to this?

10. Saul was anointed king. How did Samuel locate him?

11. The Lord gave three signs to confirm His word. What were the three signs?

12. Saul did not work out as king. Why did Samuel anoint David secretly?

Fig. 5. Bronze Spear.
Found near Jericho; 1st millennium B.C.
This Israelite spear head is the kind of equipment
King David, the warrior, would have used.

Chapter 14

DAVID

And David behaved himself wisely in all his ways;
and the Lord was with him.
1 Samuel 18:14

S aul was rejected as king. The Lord led Samuel to choose his pre-
decessor. Samuel was to go secretly to the house of Jesse in
Bethlehem where he would interview the sons of Jesse, one of
whom would become king. After Samuel had seen all the sons, he
asked, "Are here all thy children?"[1] Jesse acknowledged that there was
one more and sent for his youngest son, who was herding the sheep.
His name was David, meaning 'beloved'. When Samuel saw him, the
Lord said, "Arise, anoint him; for this is he."[2] Samuel anointed David
and the spirit of the Lord came upon David and departed from Saul.
Even so, Saul was enamored by David and made him his armor-bearer.
David played the harp for Saul which comforted him during his
tumultuous life as a king engaged in unending battles.

The Philistines prepared for battle against Israel. Goliath, a
giant, was their champion. He taunted his opponents. David witnessed this when he brought supplies to his brothers, who were serving in the army of Israel. David accepted the challenge to kill
Goliath. He confronted Goliath with a staff, a sling, and five smooth
stones—and the power of the living God. David hit him with his
first stone and used the giant's own sword to kill him. The Philistines
fled in terror.

David won battle after battle, causing Saul to become extremely
jealous to the point of wanting to kill David. The Lord was with David,
who became the pride of Israel. The man who killed Goliath was to
marry Saul's older daughter, but David claimed he was unworthy of

---

[1]1 Samuel 16:11, [2]1 Samuel 16:12

marrying the king's daughter. He did marry the king's younger daughter, Michal, who loved him very much. The required dowry was ridiculous, but David produced double what was asked. Saul's hatred and fear of David grew as David's military successes grew.

Saul's son Jonathan—David's friend—warned David that Saul was planning to kill David. Saul let up for awhile, but his restraint did not last long. When war broke out and David again was successful, Saul tried to pin David to the wall with his spear.

Michal helped David escape when messengers were sent to kill him while he slept. He went to Ramah to be with Samuel. In fact, when the messengers came close to the prophets who were with Samuel, the messengers came under God's control. Saul too was overcome by the power of God when he went after David. God held Saul prostrate on the ground all day and night, allowing David time to escape.

Jonathan helped David to find out if and when he was in danger of Saul's anger. They parted company when it was apparent that Saul intended to kill David. In his flight from Saul, David came to Ahimelech, the high priest. A servant of Saul observed Ahimelech providing bread—only holy bread was available—and reported it to Saul, hoping to cause more trouble for David.

David asked Ahimelech for a sword and was given Goliath's sword. He fled to the enemy's city—Goliath's hometown—and sought refuge among them. When the Philistines became suspicious, David pretended he was crazy to escape being killed.

David returned to Israel, living in the care of Adullam. He put together a small army of misfits who turned into a mighty army. He was concerned for his parents, who had joined him. He sought refuge for them in Moab. However, they were killed in Moab. David was told by the prophet Gad to go into hiding.

David was betrayed everywhere he went. Just as he was about to be captured, the Philistines attacked Israel, forcing Saul to turn his attention to them. Saul even entered the same cave in which David and his men were hiding. David would not let them kill Saul because God had not given the command. David talked kindly with Saul as he was departing. Saul momentarily made peace with him.

After Samuel's death, David went to the Wilderness of Paran to get away from Saul. He encountered Nabal, who rudely refused to acknowledge David's kindness in protecting Nabal's sheep.

David prepared to punish Nabal, but Abigail heard of her husband's rudeness and appeared before David on Nabal's behalf. Nabal died of other causes, and David married Abigail. David had acquired another wife—Ahinoam. His first wife, Michal, had been given to another man.

Even though David had another opportunity to kill Saul, he did not, pointing out that Saul was the Lord's anointed, and it was the Lord's responsibility to deal with him. He simply took Saul's spear and jug of water as evidence of what he could have done. Saul realized that David had spared his life and blessed him with a prophecy of greatness. They each went their own way.

David's faith waned as he fled from place to place, staying one step ahead of death. He was welcomed to the land of the Philistines by the pagan king Achish. He was given reign over the city of Ziklag, close to Israel's border, where he stayed for sixteen months.

David was ordered to join the Philistines in a battle against Israel. Saul sought advice from a spirit medium. Samuel appeared during the séance. Saul explained to Samuel his reason for seeking help. Samuel told Saul that after his defeat the next day the kingdom would belong to David.

David continued in battle, unaware that Saul was dead. David received the throne as promised by God. Saul was given death, justified before the Lord. David rose to power, becoming king over all Israel. He ordered the Ark of God brought back to Jerusalem. During its journey back, David encountered difficulties, and the Ark was placed temporarily in the house of Obed-Edom near Jerusalem. The Lord greatly blessed the household of Obed-Edom during the three months the Ark was there. David rejoiced greatly when the Ark was carried to Jerusalem. God revealed to David through the prophet Nathan that David would have a son—Solomon—who would build a temple for the Ark. David's house, his kingdom, and his throne would be established forever.[3]

David continued to defeat the enemies of Israel. It was during this period of his reign that he had a moral lapse. Bathsheba's husband, Uriah, went to battle to fight the Ammonites with King David's army under the leadership of Joab. David stayed home to rest. He sent for and committed adultery with Bathsheba. When Bathsheba discovered she was pregnant, she sent word to David, who devised a plan to hide his sin. He brought Uriah home from the army

---

[3] 2 Samuel 7:16

in an attempt to have him sleep with Bathsheba, thereby causing Uriah to believe he had impregnated her. When that plan was unsuccessful, he sent Uriah back to the frontline of battle, where he was killed.

David waited until after the proper mourning time and then took Bathsheba as his wife. Their child was born several months later. He struggled spiritually and suffered greatly for his sin. He confessed his sins against the Lord. Even though the penalty of his sins was remitted, the consequences would follow him. The baby became ill and died. David lost credence as the king of Israel. Still, he believed in God as a God of mercy and righteousness and knew that God would bless him. Bathsheba gave birth to another son, Solomon, who was destined to succeed his father as king.

When David was seventy years old and in poor health, his son Adonijah attempted to seize the throne. Adonijah held an elaborate feast, proclaiming himself king. He invited all the prominent men except Solomon, Nathan the prophet, Benaiah, and others who were loyal to David.

Bathsheba and Nathan gave the news to David and persuaded him to anoint Solomon. Bathsheba reminded David that he told her "Assuredly Solomon, thy son shall reign after me, and he shall sit upon my throne."[4] David instructed Nathan, Zadok the priest, and Benaiah to take Solomon to Gihon—a spring—on the king's mule and there to anoint him as king. David urged Solomon to be true to the Lord. He gave him other instructions and suggestions, including completion of the Temple.

David was a great statesman and an untiring general. He united the divided tribes of Israel and reigned a total of forty years, seven and a half over Judah from Hebron and thirty-three over the whole Kingdom of Israel. His reign extended from ca. 1010 to 970 B.C. David died and was buried in Jerusalem.

Kubal was a man of courage. He joined his country's army and was sent to Khorsica to help that young country set up a government to serve her people. Kubal fought bravely and was admired by those around him. However, the constant slaying by the troops did not accomplish his country's desired goals.

---

[4] 1 Kings 1:17

Kubal developed battle fatigue. During a lapse in his moral judgment, he fled to the side of the enemy and sought refuge in a remote village. He was taken in by a family who admired his courage and fell for his smooth talk. Kubal ultimately married the eldest daughter of the family.

David was the most powerful king to rule Israel. In addition to being a soldier and statesman, David was a poet. He is credited with the beautiful dirge found in 2 Samuel 1, as well as those chapters ascribed to him in the Book of Psalms.

Kubal lived happily ever after—until his own country's army tracked him down twenty years later for desertion. Kubal's family lacked the courage—and legal authority—to defend his actions of twenty years before. Kubal's fate is up to the courts in his country. Was he justified in switching his allegiance?

Kubal, like David, was brave and willing to confront the enemy. Both men suffered moral breakdowns. David knew that even though God forgave him his sins he would suffer the consequences of sin. He was a great statesman. He followed God's command. Kubal has yet to acknowledge the existence of God.

He is the tower of salvation for his king:
and sheweth mercy to his anointed, unto David
and his seed for evermore.
2 Samuel 22:51

Suggested Scripture Readings

1 Samuel 16 – 1 Kings 2; 1 Chronicles 18:14; Jeremiah 33:17.

Study Questions

1. Samuel interviewed the sons of Jesse. Why was he interested in them?

2. David's name meant 'beloved'. Why was he not interviewed with his brothers?

3. David killed Goliath. Why was David on the battlefield?

4. Saul was jealous of David. What was David doing to cause Saul concern?

5. Saul's son and daughter helped David. How was David able to escape from Saul in Ramah?

6. David was given holy bread by the high priest. When is bread considered holy?

7. Saul entered a cave in which David was hiding. Why did David not kill Saul when he had the opportunity?

8. Nabal refused to acknowledge David's kindness. What occurred as a result of their encounter?

9. David stayed home from battle to rest. What great sin did he commit during this time?

10. The first child of David and Bathsheba died. What happened to their second son?

Chapter 15

NATHAN

⌐⎯⌐

And Nathan said to the king,
Go, do all that is in thine heart; for the Lord is with thee.
2 Samuel 7:3

Nathan—'gift of God'—was a prophet in King David's court. He acted as the royal advisor to King David.

During this era, the Israeli Ark of God—the Ark of the Covenant—was a direct manifestation of God. Containing tablets of law, the Ark was kept inside a tent behind curtains with an attendant guarding it. It was used whenever the people felt the need for divine power; for instance, it led them into battle, through the desert, and around the walls of Jericho.

David felt it was wrong for the Ark to be kept in a tent when he was living in a fine dwelling. He consulted with Nathan about building a Temple in which to house the Ark. Nathan thought that would be appropriate. He assumed God had approved and, therefore, did not consult with Him.

God promptly told Nathan that David would not be the one to build the Temple for the Lord. God said that a tent was appropriate at the time because the children of Israel had been wandering since their exodus from Egypt. After they settled in one place and God established a human leadership over Israel, they could build a Temple in His name.

The Lord told Nathan that he would make a covenant with David in which he promised that David would have a son—Solomon—who would build the Temple. Solomon's throne would be forever. God would correct him when he sinned, but God's mercy on Solomon would not cease. He further promised Nathan that David's house, kingdom, and throne would be established forever.

The prophets of Israel had a way of reminding the kings of their moral failings. Nathan thus trapped David during one of David's spiritual struggles by telling him the parable of the poor man's ewe: A rich man with many sheep was unwilling to use one of his own lambs for food when he was preparing dinner for company. Instead, he took a lamb from a poor man and slaughtered it. When Nathan asked David his judgment on the matter, David angrily declared that the rich man should restore fourfold that which he had taken. In fact, he felt that the rich man deserved to die for what he had done. David was better able to judge sin in others than in himself.

Nathan pointed out to David that he was the guilty one for having taken Bathsheba from her husband and then having him killed to hide the crime. Nathan added that God was forgiving, and David would not die. But the consequences of his sin would follow him: The baby would die; his son Amnon would be murdered; his son Absalom would be murdered; his son Adonijah would be executed; and David's wives would be publicly violated.

When David and Bathsheba's son Solomon was born, God named him Jedidiah, meaning 'beloved of Jehovah'. God's will in this matter was expressed through Nathan

As time passed, Nathan was intent on seeing God's word carried out and Solomon anointed as king. He coached Bathsheba to alert the ailing seventy-year-old David of Adonijah's attempt to succeed his father as king. Because of Nathan's intervention, David instructed him, along with Zadok the priest and Benaiah, the general, to take Solomon to Gihon—a spring—on David's own mule and anoint him as king.

The words of David in Psalm 51, which lamented his spiritual relapse with Bathsheba, were written after Nathan exposed him for committing adultery with Bathsheba and having her husband Uriah murdered. In the Psalm, David pours out his brokenness, confesses, asks for mercy, begs to be cleansed, and praises God for His forgiveness.

Ben wanted a new car. His old one ran okay, but all of his friends had late models and often teased him about his out-of-date pile of junk. He spent what little time he had between his two jobs looking at and driving demonstrators of cars he would like to own.

He did not mention new cars to his young wife Sarah because he knew the stress she was already under to make ends meet. She was having problems in her seventh month of pregnancy and was supposed to be getting bed rest. Having to quit her job had made their financial crisis even more severe.

Ben was so taken with the sharp, red convertible that he was test-driving that he drove it home to let Sarah see it. If she were up to it, he would take her for a spin. He heard a siren as he approached their house and was shocked to have the ambulance, its lights flashing, cut in front of him and stop at his house.

Ben panicked. He pulled in behind the ambulance and raced into the house. "Please, Lord, don't let anything happen to her!" he begged.

Sarah was standing by the door as he barged in behind the ambulance team. "I think it's either a heart attack or stroke," she called to the medics, pointing toward the living room floor. Ben caught a glimpse of his mother-in-law, crumpled beside the sofa. She had come to help Sarah with the housework to enable her to get the bed rest recommended by the doctor.

"Oh, Sarah," cried Ben, unable to say anything else.

The medics quickly assessed the situation and made the decision to transport his mother-in-law to the hospital for testing and expert care. "She's had a slight heart attack but should be all right," they told Sarah.

"That fancy red convertible behind the ambulance looks like something you'd like to have some day, Sweetie," observed Sarah as she followed the stretcher to the ambulance. "I wonder who the ambulance chaser is."

"I don't know," replied Ben. "But if you'll ride in the ambulance with your mother, I'll meet you at the hospital."

We have a tendency to live our daily lives according to our own wishes, not giving a second thought to God's will—until disaster strikes. Then we are jolted back to the realization that God is in control. We must invite Him into our hearts and ask His guidance in our daily decision-making. Without Him, we are lost.

Therefore now let it please thee to bless the house of thy servant,
that it may continue forever before thee:for thou,
O Lord God, hast spoken it: and with thy
blessing let the house of thy servant
be blessed forever.
2 Samuel 7:29

Suggested Scripture Readings

2 Samuel 7; 12; 1 Kings 1; 1 Chronicles 17; 29:29; 2 Chronicles 9:29; 29:25; Psalm 51.

Study Questions

1. Biblical names have meaning. What does *Nathan* mean?

2. Nathan was a prophet in David's court. What did he do other than foreseeing the future?

3. Nathan told David to build a temple for the Ark. What did Nathan neglect to do before advising David?

4. God said that the tent was appropriate for housing the Ark. What were His reasons?

5. The Ark was a manifestation of God. What were some of the ways it was used?

6. God told Nathan that He would make a covenant with David? What did God promise David?

7. Nathan caught David in a moral crime. How did he do this?

8. Nathan said that God forgave David. What would happen to David as a result of his sin?

9. David was old and sick. How was Solomon anointed?

10. David wrote about his sins. Where in Scripture is this lament found?

Fig. 6. Bowl.
Ca. 1000 B.C. Typical of bowls used for food
during the time of Saul and David.

Chapter 16

SOLOMON

*Wisdom and knowledge is granted unto thee; and I will give thee
riches and wealth, and honor, such as none of the kings have had
that have been before thee, neither shall there any
after thee have the like.*
2 Chronicles 1:12

The Scripture is not clear as to whether Solomon was David
and Bathsheba's second child (1 Samuel 12) or whether there
were intervening children.[1] He was also known as Jedidiah,
meaning in Hebrew, '*Yahweh's* beloved'.[2]

David's son Adonijah tried to succeed David, supported by
General Joab and the priest Abiathar. Bathsheba insisted that David
keep his promise that Solomon would be anointed. With the help of
the prophet Nathan, the priest Zadok, and Benaiah from the royal
guard, Solomon was anointed king. Solomon saw Adonijah and Joab
as continued threats and had them executed.

Solomon embellished the role of the king. New political
boundaries replaced the old accepted tribal boundaries. He orga-
nized Israel into twelve districts and appointed a governor for each.
Expanded trade routes and involvement in trade enterprises enriched
his kingdom. The expansion of Solomon's kingdom brought great
wealth, due in part to his great wisdom.

Solomon acquired 700 wives, including Edomite, Hittite,
Moabite, and Phoenician women.[3] He built a palace and the Temple
in Jerusalem. His elaborate palace took thirteen years to build and
the Temple took seven years. At the same time, many cities and
fortresses were developed. He collaborated with King Hiram (of

---

[1] 1 Chronicles 3:5, [2] 2 Samuel 12:25, [3] 1 Kings 11:1

Tyre) in building a navy and organizing large fleets for the purpose of trading.

When God appeared to Solomon at Gibeon and asked him what he desired most, Solomon asked for an understanding heart. God promised him wisdom, as well as riches, honor, and a long life if he would walk with God. God granted him wisdom—an understanding mind.[4] He was able to use his wisdom to develop his kingdom, increase his wealth, and settle disputes. An example of Solomon's wisdom was the manner in which he settled a dispute between two harlots who were arguing over a baby. When Solomon offered to split the child in two, the true mother asked to spare the child, even if it meant that she had to give the baby up to the other woman. Solomon's wisdom brought him respect throughout the land.

The Queen of Sheba was overwhelmed by Solomon's wisdom. She traveled to his kingdom for the purpose of posing difficult questions. He answered them all wisely, thus winning her confidence, respect, and more wealth.

Solomon's wealth—resulting from heavy taxation of his people—ultimately led to his downfall. His vast wealth resulted in lavish spending and the onset of religious decadence. Along with the plentiful acquisition of gold, silver, and other opulence, Solomon turned to idolatry. His vast knowledge and worldliness brought criticism from those who wished him ill. His dealings with outsiders brought about unacceptable practices. His enemies included Hadad, an Edomite prince,[5] Rezon of Zobah,[6] and Jeroboam of Israel.[7] God warned him that his kingdom would be taken from him and given to one of his servants because of his decadent practices.

Construction of the Temple began in the fourth year of Solomon's reign. Its dimensions and elaborate plans are described in 1 Kings 6. All the furnishings were made by Solomon except the Ark of the Covenant, which was brought from the tabernacle. He selected 70,000 men to carry the materials for the Temple. In addition, he had 80,000 stonecutters and 3,600 men to supervise the work. He sent a request to Hiram for timber—cedars—and a craftsman. Hiram promised the wood in exchange for wheat, barley, oil, and wine.

Upon completion of the Temple, Solomon gave a lengthy prayer of dedication. He asked God to accept his prayer. He asked

---

[4]1 Kings 3:5-9, [5]1 Kings 11:14, [6]1 Kings 11:23, [7]1 Kings 11:26

God to shower the priests who would serve in the Temple with grace and joy, and finally—based on God's love for David (Solomon's father)—he asked God's favor for himself.

When Solomon finished praying, God sent fire from heaven to consume the burnt offerings and sacrifices. "The glory of the Lord filled the Temple." The dedication and feast lasted seven days.

Although the Song of Solomon has been given numerous meanings, most prevalent, an exchange of love between a man and woman, a higher level of meaning interprets it as the love between God and man, God and Israel, or Christ and the church.

The book The Wisdom of Solomon is found in the Apocrypha. The first part teaches the destiny of the righteous and the wicked and the praise of wisdom. The second part seeks to lure the Jews of Egypt back to their ancestral faith.

Solomon reigned for about forty years from around 965 B.C. until his death ca. 928 B.C. He was succeeded by his son Rehoboam. Matthew 1:6-7 lists him as an ancestor of Christ.

———

Solomon asked for and received the gifts of wisdom, joy, and wealth. He used them to glorify God up to a point and received abundant blessings from God. From that point on, he bogged down in unacceptable practices. The following parable further illustrates what happens when we misuse God's provision.

The wise old school teacher ruled with authority. He presented his lessons with clarity and made certain his students understood the object of his lessons before he dismissed them for the day. He showed patience and understanding when he had to repeat his lesson over and over for a few students who were inattentive as well as disinterested.

The outstanding student each year was awarded a scholarship to a prestigious university for further study. The son of the wealthy town merchant was in the old teacher's class, not because he was academically talented, but because his father bribed the school superintendent. The young student seldom did his assigned lessons, believing that his father's wealth would buy him the coveted scholarship at the end of the year.

When the time came for the awards ceremony at the end of the school term, a hush fell over the crowded auditorium. The wealthy parents sat near the front, confident that their son would receive the honor. The widowed mother of a rather timid student who spent all of his time studying sat near the door in the back of the auditorium.

The tired, old teacher walked to the front of the stage and beckoned the two boys to stand. "In my hand," he began, "I hold two envelopes. One contains a scholarship to the university. The other contains a copy of our last examination. Whichever of you can answer correctly this question will have earned the scholarship. The other will receive a copy of the examination from which I again ask this question:How do you spell the capital of Greece, R-o-a-m or R-o-m-e?"

The son of the wealthy merchant quickly shouted out, "R-o-m-e!"

In a soft, but steady voice, the timid young student said, "Athens, A-t-h-e-n-s."

The stunned audience gasped and then cheered as the old teacher handed the coveted scholarship to the rightful recipient.

God gives each of us spiritual gifts to use to magnify Him. To God be the glory. Great things He has done!

And Solomon slept with his fathers, and he was buried in the city of David his father, and Rehoboam his son reigned in his stead.
2 Chronicles 9:31

Suggested Scripture Readings

1 Kings 1 – 12; 2 Chronicles 1 – 9.

Study Questions

1. Solomon was also known as Jedidiah, meaning 'beloved'. In what ways did he live up to his name?

2. Adonijah tried to succeed his father as king. Why was Solomon anointed?

3. Solomon did many things as king. How did he expand his kingdom?

4. Solomon acquired many wives. Why did he do this and why was he criticized?

5. Solomon built a palace and Temple. Why did it take so long?

6. Solomon had great wisdom. How did he use his wisdom?

7. God asked Solomon what he desired most. What all did God grant Solomon?

8. The Queen of Sheba visited Solomon. How did she react to him?

9. Solomon's opulence brought disaster. What happened?

10. Solomon asked God to accept his prayer of dedication. What did God do?

Chapter 17

ELIJAH

—◦——◦—

Behold, I will send you Elijah the prophet
before the coming of the great and
dreadful day of the Lord.
Malachi 4:5

During the first half of the ninth century B.C., a Tishbite from Gilead was sent by God as a prophet to the people of Israel. Dressed in leather, indicating that he may have hailed from a shepherd family in Transjordan, Elijah would spend his life fighting Baal. He proclaimed the Lord as a supreme, omniscient judge who, in due time, will respond to the indiscretions of the people.

The emphasis of Elijah's life as a prophet of God is found in four stories within the Holy Scripture:Elijah prophesies a drought to punish Israel for her turn to idolatry;[1] Elijah prophesies doom to King Ahab and his family for the murder of Naboth;[2] Elijah prophesies doom to King Ahaziah, who fell and became ill;[3] and Elisha becomes Elijah's servant, inheriting two-thirds of his master's spirit.[4]

Elijah told King Ahab that a drought was imminent as punishment to the nation for its idol worship. He became Ahab's number one enemy and was forced to run for his life. God told Elijah to hide by the brook Cherith, where he could drink from the brook and eat the food brought to him by the ravens. After some time at the brook, its waters dried up because of the drought, and he had to leave.

---

[1]1 Kings 16:29-19:180, [2]1 Kings 21, [3]2 Kings 1:2-2:17, [4]1 Kings 19:19-21; 2 Kings 2:1-18

God instructed Elijah to go to Zarephath, where he would meet a widow who would care for him. As he approached the gate of the city, he saw the woman gathering sticks. He asked her for a drink of water. As she was going to get the water, he told her to bring him a bit of bread. She informed Elijah that she had only a handful of meal and a little oil. She had been gathering firewood to bake one last meal for herself and her son before they both died of starvation.

Elijah told her to do as she planned, but to make him a little cake first and then make one for herself and her son. She did as he asked. The meal and oil lasted until the end of the drought, according to the word of the Lord spoken to Elijah.

The widow's son became ill and died. She blamed Elijah. Elijah took the boy up to the loft and laid him on the bed. He asked God to bring life back to the boy. He stretched out over the child three times, asking God to let the child's soul return into him. The child was revived, and Elijah took him back to his mother, saying, "See, thy son liveth."

The widow said, "Now by this I know that thou art a man of God, and that the word of the Lord in thy mouth is truth."[5]

Three years later, the Lord instructed Elijah to go back to King Ahab, and the drought would end. There was a terrible famine in Samaria. Ahab and Obadiah had gone in search of food for the animals. Obadiah was the one who had saved one hundred prophets of the Lord from being killed while Ahab's wife, Jezebel, was murdering all she could find.

Elijah told Obadiah to let Ahab know he was back. Obadiah was afraid Ahab would kill him if the "Spirit of the Lord" carried Elijah away before Ahab saw him. Elijah promised Obadiah he would remain, and they arranged a meeting place.

When they met, Ahab accused Elijah of being a troublemaker for Israel. Elijah reminded him that he—Ahab—was the troublemaker for forsaking the Lord's commandments and reverting to Baal-worship.

Ahab sent all the Israelites and the prophets to meet at Mount Carmel. Elijah told them that they had to choose between the Lord and Baal. Elijah would prepare one bull as a sacrifice and the 450 prophets of Ahab would prepare one bull. They would call on their gods for fire and Elijah would call on the Lord for fire. The people agreed to accept the God who answered the call as their God.

[5]1 Kings 17:24

The rituals performed by Ahab's prophets did not work. Elijah repaired the altar of the Lord. He used twelve stones, representing the tribes of the sons of Jacob. He prepared a trench around the altar to hold water, arranged the wood, cut the meat, and laid it on the wood.

At the time of the offering of the evening sacrifice, Elijah prayed to the Lord to send fire. The fire of the Lord fell immediately from heaven and consumed everything, including the stones, wood, and water. The people fell down and said, "The Lord, He is the God."

At last the rain came, ending the drought and famine after the people acknowledged Jehovah as their God. Elijah ascended Mount Carmel to pray. He prayed until one of his servants told him the clouds were gathering. Elijah sent Ahab on to Jezreel in his chariot. Elijah ran in front of the chariot the twenty miles to the royal house in Jezreel.

Ahab told Jezebel all that had transpired. She vowed to kill Elijah. Elijah immediately ran for his life. He left his servant at Beersheba, and went into the wilderness. He lay down under a juniper tree and went to sleep. An angel wakened him and told him to eat and drink of the freshly baked cake and water that were there. He ate and lay down again. The angel wakened him the second time, telling him to eat and drink so that he would have strength for the forty days and nights journey to Horeb (Sinai), the mount of God.

He found a cave and lived there. The Lord came to him in the cave. Elijah was so wrapped up in his own self-importance that he would not obey the Lord. God sent wind, an earthquake, and fire to jolt Elijah out of the cave. Finally, after the fire, Elijah heard a voice ask, "What doest thou here, Elijah?"[6] Elijah went to the entrance of the cave and exalted the Lord.

The Lord told him to return to the Wilderness of Damascus where he would anoint Hazael as King of Syria; Jehu as king over Israel; and Elisha as prophet to succeed Elijah. The three of them would slay all but the seven thousand who had not bowed down to Baal. Elijah left to find Elisha and cast his mantle upon him, a sign that Elisha was to be his successor. Elisha followed him and became his personal servant.

When Jezebel committed evil works to acquire a vineyard that Ahab wanted for a vegetable garden next to his palace property,

---

[6] 1 Kings 19:9

Elijah intervened. He predicted that Ahab and his male descendants would be slain, and that Jezebel too would meet her demise. When Ahab humbled himself before the Lord, the Lord prolonged Jezebel's death until after Ahab's death so that he would not have to witness the brutality.

King Ahaziah fell and injured himself. He sent for the pagan god Baal-Zebub to heal him. Elijah met the messengers and sent them back to Ahaziah with a rebuke for asking for healing from a pagan god. Ahaziah sent fifty men to bring Elijah to him for a reprimand.

God destroyed the captain and the fifty men. A second group was sent, but they too met the same fate. The third captain pleaded with Elijah for mercy. The angel of the Lord told Elijah to go to Ahaziah. Elijah told the king that he would die because he had consulted a pagan god. Ahaziah died and was succeeded by his brother Jehoram.

The time had come for Elijah's ministry to end. Elisha went with him to Bethel, Jericho, and Jordan. As they approached the Jordan River, Elijah struck the waters with his mantle, and the two crossed over. Elijah is credited with performing eight miracles. Sixteen are attributed to Elisha.

As they continue their walk, they were separated by a chariot of fire and horses of fire. As Elijah was swept up into heaven, Elisha cried out, "My father, my father, the chariot of Israel and its horsemen,"[7] and he saw Elijah no more.

Elijah was a zealot of the Lord, fighting idolatry and injustice. Yet he could not be coerced into leaving the cave. In the same way, storms, earthquakes, and fires cannot move massive mounds of sinfulness within us. Only the gentle persuasion of God's love has the power to coerce us into shedding our mantles of sin.

A loving father bade farewell to his only son at the gate leading up to the university campus. He handed the young man a Bible as he braced himself for the dreaded goodbye. The young man, expecting a handshake and a check, stuck the book in his backpack and headed for the old building which housed the men's dormitory. He stepped

[7]2 Kings 2:12

from the grace of Christian love into the vileness of a smoke-filled room of skepticism and rebellion.

The Bible fell to the floor when he threw his backpack on the bed in the corner. An envelope slipped out of the Bible and slid unnoticed underneath the bed. Someone inadvertently kicked the Bible, and it too slipped out of sight. The young man's initial reaction was, "I don't belong here."

The smoldering mattress went unnoticed until it burst into flames. The crowd evacuated the room quickly, unaware that the latest arrival was trapped in the corner by the ensuing heat and smoke. They watched from the ground while the old house succumbed to the fire.

The young man would never read the persuasive words of love written by his father. He could only pray as the whirlwind of fire lifted him to new heights. Just as the water from the fireman's hose extinguishes the flames, so does agape love abolish sin.

And he took the mantle of Elijah that fell from him, and smote the waters, and said, "Where is the Lord God of Elijah? and when he had smitten the waters, they parted hither and thither, and Elisha went over.
2 Kings 2:14

Suggested Scripture Reading

1 Kings 17 - 21:17-29; 2 Kings 1 – 3:11; 9:36 - 10:10; 17; 2 Chronicles 21:12; Malachi 4:5.

Study Questions

1. Elijah's life as a prophet includes four main phenomena. What were they?

2. Elijah warned King Ahab of a drought. Why were the people being punished?

3. Elijah fled to the brook Cherith. Why was he hiding?

4. God sent Elijah to Zarephath. What was he instructed to do there?

5. It was three years before Elijah returned to King Ahab. What was to happen upon his return?

6. Obadiah was afraid. Why did he think Ahab would kill him?

7. Ahab sent all the Israelites to Mount Carmel. What happened there?

8. The fire of the Lord consumed everything. What did this prove to the people?

9. Elijah ascended Mount Carmel to pray. Why was he praying?

10. Elijah fled one more time. How did the Lord jolt Elijah from the cave?

11. Ahaziah became ill. Why did Elijah rebuke him?

12. Elijah passed his mantle to Elisha. How did Elijah ascend into heaven?

Fig. 7. Tall Roman Storage Vessel.
Used from 100 – 400 A.D.
During a drought, Elijah asked a widow in Zarephath
for food. She had very little in her grain jar, yet he told her to
make him a small cake to show faith. He promised that the
remaining flour would be replenished miraculously
until the drought ended.

Chapter 18

ELISHA

And Elisha saw it, and he cried, My father, my father,
the chariot of Israel, and the horsemen thereof.
And he saw him no more: and he took hold of
his own clothes, and rent them in two pieces.
2 Kings 2:12

The Lord told the prophet Elijah to return to the wilderness of Damascus where he was to anoint Hazael as king over Syria; Jehu as king over Israel; and Elisha to replace him as prophet. Elijah found Elisha, son of Shaphat, plowing in the field and threw his mantle around him. Elisha asked if he could bid his father and mother farewell before he left with Elijah. Elijah gave him permission, but warned him not to ignore the fact that he had been anointed. After an elaborate feast, Elisha followed Elijah and became his personal servant.

When the time had come for the Lord to take Elijah into heaven by a whirlwind, the two traveled to Bethel, on to Jericho, and then to the Jordan River. Elijah parted the waters of the Jordan with his mantle so they could cross on dry land. Elijah asked Elisha what he wanted before Elijah was taken away. Elisha requested a double portion of Elijah's spirit to be upon Elisha. Elijah said it would be so if Elisha were a witness to his being taken into heaven. As they continued their journey, a chariot of fire and horses of fire appeared, parting the two, and Elijah went up by a whirlwind into heaven.

The double portion is the right of the first-born son. Elisha simply wanted to be worthy of being Elijah's successor. It may not be mere coincidence to note that Elisha performed sixteen recorded miracles, double the eight performed by Elijah.

Elisha took up the mantle of Elijah that had fallen from him and went to the bank of the Jordan. He struck the waters with the mantle saying, "Where is the Lord God of Elijah?"And the waters parted. Elisha crossed over. The sons of the prophets in Jericho saw him and bowed down before him. They persuaded him to let them send fifty men to find Elijah, although Elisha knew they would not find him.

From this point forward, Elisha performed a series of miracles in an attempt to lead Israel away from idolatry and back to the living God. He threw salt into the fountain at Jericho to cleanse the water so that it would never again cause death or barren land.

As Elisha was going into Bethel, a group of children mocked him, calling him 'bald head'. Elisha was bald and carried a staff. He cursed them in the name of the Lord. Two female bears came out of the woods and mauled forty-two of the children.

Elisha retraced the steps of Elijah in Jericho and Bethel before going on to Mount Carmel and Samaria. The people at Jericho were blessed for treating him with respect. The young people at Bethel received a curse for treating him with disrespect.

Jehosaphat, along with the kings of Israel and Edom, sought Elisha's help when the army ran out of water. Elisha told them to consult their own idolatrous prophets. They insisted, and Elisha reluctantly agreed to consult the Lord. As a musician played, Elisha felt the power of the Lord come upon him. He predicted that water—not rain—would come into the valley, and the Moabites would be defeated. The water resembled blood in the sunlight. The king of Moab offered his eldest son as a burnt offering. The men of Israel were so stunned by this that they hurried away from him and returned to their own land.

A miraculous provision of oil was given to a widow who was about to have her sons taken away from her by creditors during a famine. Elisha told her to fill as many vessels as she could find, using the pot of oil she had in her house. She sold the oil to pay off her debt and support her family.

A Shunamitte woman recognized Elisha as a man of God and provided him with hospitality each time he passed through Shunem. Even though her husband was old, Elisha—at the suggestion of his servant Gehazi—told her she would bear a son. When the son was older, he became ill. He went to the field to tell his father, who had him carried back to his mother. The child died later that day. She put his body in Elisha's chamber and set out for Mount Carmel to find Elisha.

Elisha saw her approaching and sent Gehazi to meet her. She went directly to Elisha, who was unaware that the child had died. She indirectly accused him of giving her a son and then taking the child from her. Elisha thought the child was ill. Gehazi went to her house to see the child and reported back to Elisha that the child was dead. When Elisha arrived at the house, he stretched out over the child three times and life came back into the boy.

Elisha's next miracle took place when stew being cooked for the sons of the prophets was inadvertently poisoned from using toxic gourds as one of the ingredients. Elisha added flour to the pot, making the stew safe to eat.

Another miracle occurred when Elisha fed one hundred men with twenty small loaves of barley bread and some grain.

Elisha proved he did not have to be present for a miracle to occur. A Jewish girl who was a captive servant living in the home of Naaman, the commander of the Syrian army, suggested that he meet with Elisha to be healed of leprosy. Naaman took a letter of introduction from the King of Syria to the King of Israel, requesting healing. The King of Israel was angry and refused the request, thinking it was an attempt to attack Israel.

Elisha heard of the situation and sent word for Naaman to wash in the Jordan River seven times. Naaman was angry because he had expected a more dramatic approach. He complained and said the waters of his native Damascus were superior to the Jordan. His servants persuaded him to give it a try, and he was completely healed. Elisha's greedy servant Gehazi secretly accepted the gifts refused by Elisha. As a result, Gehazi contracted the leprosy of Naaman.

Elisha miraculously recovered an axe-head that was lost in the Jordan by throwing a stick into the river, causing the axe-head to float. The distressed owner was able to retrieve it.

Elisha was revealing the secret battle plans of the King of Syria to the King of Israel. When the King of Syria found out, he determined he could capture Elisha by surrounding the city of Dothan where Elisha was staying. Elisha asked the Lord to strike the enemy with blindness and lead the Israelites to Samaria. He ordered the King of Israel to feed the blind enemy soldiers instead of killing them.

The King of Israel was going to kill Elisha for causing a famine. Elisha heard that the king and his messengers were on the way. When they met, Elisha told the king that fine flour and barley would be sold the next day at the gate of Samaria.

Four lepers entered the Syrian camp and helped themselves to its contents. They decided to tell the king so that they would not be punished. The people of Israel took all the spoils from the Syrian camp and the famine was over.

Elisha told the Shunammite woman whose son he had restored to life to go to another land because there would be a seven-year famine. She took her family into the land of the Philistines. Elisha's servant, Gehazi, was in the king's court when the woman returned and asked that her house and land be returned to her. The king heard what Elisha had done for her—reviving her son—and ordered her house, property, and the produce raised in the fields for the seven years restored to her.

Elisha prophesied that Ben-Hadad, King of Syria, would die—not from illness, but because Hazael would murder him. Hazael would become King of Syria, inflicting pain and suffering on the people.

Elisha sent one of the sons of the prophets to anoint Jehu as King of Israel, commissioning him to destroy the house of Ahab. This responsibility had been passed on from Elijah to Elisha. Jehu carried out the Word of the Lord as spoken to Elijah.

When Elisha became ill and was dying, Joash visited him, using the same words that Elisha had used when Elijah was passing:"O my father, my father, the chariots of Israel and their horseman." Elisha told Joash to take a bow and arrow, shoot one arrow, and strike the ground with the other arrows. This act signified deliverance from Syria. Joash struck the ground only three times. If he had struck the ground five or six times, it would have eliminated Syria's threat on them.

Elisha died and was buried. He reigned from ca. 850 – 800 B.C., during the reigns of Joram, Jehu, Jehoahaz, and Joash. He was a man of wisdom and a miracle-worker for Israel as well as for individuals. His ministry depicts God's power over nature—Baal-worshipers—

as well as in the economic and social strata of the time. We may never understand why some things happen, but we do know that God is in control.

The old man tottered down the dusty path, his bald head shiny with sweat. The end of his staff caught between two uneven rocks, causing him to lurch forward. He would have fallen, had it not been for the rock wall that separated the path from the steep incline down the side of the mountain. He was on his way to worship at the temple below. He no longer relied on the carved images that adorned the temple to send rain when the crops were wilting, fill his lamp when the wick went out, or provide food when the grain sack was empty. He had found a new God.

The missionary from the other side of the giant waters that separated his country from the rest of the world came once a year to teach him and the other villagers about this new God. When the missionary was not there, the old man had accepted the responsibility to feed the minds of his friends with God-given food.

As he leaned against the wall to catch his breath, a group of noisy youngsters rounded the curve in the path. When they saw him, they started yelling obscenities and ridiculing his baldness. "All that foolishness in your head made your hair fall out, old man. If your God is so great, why hasn't He given you a horse and chariot to ride instead of making you stumble and fall?"

The cobra that struck the youngster had been in the path all the time the young people were mocking the old man. They had forgotten the constant warnings of their parents to be on the lookout for snakes. The shriek of the lad echoed down the valley as the terrified youths joined hands to make a seat to carry their friend back to his hut. The old man pushed a heavy boulder off the wall onto the head of the hooded viper, crushing it and holding its thrashing body in place.

The world is filled with evil. God did not necessarily cause the snake to be in the path at that particular time. But He does take care of His own. He worked miracles through Elisha to help individuals in need of food and healing. He worked miracles through Elisha to solve the political and economic problems of Israel, most of which were caused by the people worshiping idols instead of their Lord. He works through you and me to lead others to eternal salvation. He takes care of those who accept Him as their personal Lord and Savior.

And he answered, "Thou shalt not smite them:wouldest thou smite those whom thou hast taken captive with thy sword and with thy bow?Set bread and water before them, that they may eat and drink, and go to their master."
2 Kings 6:22

Suggested Scripture

1 Kings 19:16-21; 2 Kings 2 – 9; 13:14 – 21.

Study Questions

1. Elisha was working in the field when Elijah threw his mantle around him. What did Elisha request?

2. Elijah and Elisha traveled to Jordan. How did they cross the river?

3. Elisha requested a double portion of Elijah's spirit. What did he mean?

4. Elisha parted the waters of the Jordan. What was his real reason for doing this?

5. Elisha performed miracles. What purpose did the miracles serve?

6. The army needed water. Why was Elisha reluctant to consult the Lord?

7. The Shunamitte woman returned to her house after the famine. Why did the king reimburse her?

8. Jehu was anointed. What was his commission?

9. Elisha told Joash to shoot an arrow. What was the significance of this?

10. Elisha was a man of wisdom. What does his ministry depict?

Fig. 8. Zoomorphic Vessel.
Middle Eastern zoomorphic vessel found in Israel, 1200 – 800 B.C.
It is the figure of a cow; perhaps an oil storage container.

Chapter 19

MORDECAI

Then the king's servants, which were in the king's gate,
said unto Mordecai, "Why transgressest thou
the king's commandment?"
Esther 3:3

Mordecai, a Benjamite, had been taken captive in Jerusalem and was living in Shushan as a servant in the king's palace. It is believed that King Ahasuerus was Xerxes, the son of Darius the Great. He reigned from 486 to 465 B.C.

Mordecai was caring for Esther, his uncle's daughter who was orphaned. Esther was taken to the palace as a possible candidate for the king's harem. She did not let anyone know she was a Jew. Mordecai checked on her each day to make certain she was all right. The king loved Esther above all the other women and made her his queen.

Mordecai worked at the king's gate. He overheard two of the king's servants plotting to kill the king. He told Esther, who—crediting Mordecai—let the king know. The men were hanged, and it was written in the king's chronicles.

Haman, another worker at the palace, received a promotion that put him over all others. Everyone bowed down to him except Mordecai. The law did not forbid people to show respect to authority. It did forbid worship of any but God. Haman was angry with Mordecai, especially when he found out Mordecai was a Jew. The king gave Haman the authority to write letters and to sign them with the king's signature ring. Haman tricked the king into making a law which would kill all Jews.

When Mordecai found out, he mourned and put on sackcloth and ashes. Esther heard of Mordecai's mourning and found out the reason. Mordecai sent word to Esther that it was her duty to go to the king and tell him the situation; for if all Jews were to die, so would she.

It was the custom that no one—not even the queen—could approach the king without being summoned. Anyone doing so would be put to death unless the king extended his golden scepter.

Esther sent word to Mordecai to gather all the Jews in Shushan and fast for three days. On the third day, Esther approached the king and was received by him. He asked what he could do for her.

Esther suggested to the king that he invite Haman to a banquet she was preparing. Haman attended and boasted afterward to his family. He was enraged that Mordecai did not bow to him as he entered the palace and when he departed.

Haman was invited again for the next day. His wife and friends suggested he make a gallows on which to hang Mordecai.

The king could not sleep that night. He asked his servants to read to him from his chronicles. They came to the page where it was written that two of his servants plotted his death and Mordecai informed the king. The king asked how Mordecai had been honored for this. The servants answered that nothing had been done.

Haman was in the court and the king called him in. The king asked Haman what would be a fitting way to honor a man. Haman—all the time thinking the king was referring to him—suggested dressing the man in the king's apparel, putting him on the king's horse, putting the king's crown on his head, and letting him ride thus through the streets of the city. He was mortified when he had to honor Mordecai in this way and went home to complain to his wife and friends. Even so, the king's servants came to escort him back to the second banquet Esther had prepared.

At the banquet, the king asked Esther what she desired. Esther told the king of Haman's trickery and how she and all the Jews were to be killed under the new law set by Haman. The king rose and went into his garden. When he came back in, Haman was on Esther's bed, begging for mercy. This really infuriated the king.

A servant told the king about the gallows Haman had built to hang Mordecai. The king told them to hang Haman on the gallows—which they did.

The king gave all Haman's belongings to Esther. He took back his signature ring from Haman and gave it to Mordecai. He told Esther and Mordecai to reverse the laws Haman had written to kill all Jews. Mordecai was honored as one of the royal family. He became an influential confidant of the king. There is no date nor mention of Mordecai's death. "And the world passeth away, and the least thereof:but he that doeth the will of God abideth forever."[1]

We are always sad when evil reigns, but, as Christians, we should reach out to God's throne of grace for mercy in times of need. Was it in God's plan for the king to read the pages in his chronicles detailing Mordecai's actions to save the king from assassination? Mordecai and Esther hid the fact that they were Jews, knowing that they would be rejected by the king and his court. The following parable illustrates what happens when we avoid the truth.

A young man and woman had been seeing each other for several months. They enjoyed the same leisure-time activities and had several mutual friends. They avoided talking about God and their religious beliefs even though her parents were practicing Christians. They were doing just fine without God, and, although she often dreamed of walking down the aisle in a beautiful white wedding gown, she did not want to risk losing his friendship.

He, on the other hand, knew that there must be a God somewhere, or he would not have survived his last overdose of drugs. He even remembered promising God that he would never do it again if He just got him through one more time. Yet he had not told her because he was afraid of losing her friendship. They continued their relationship, knowing that they should divulge their uncertainties to one another.

It was Mother's Day, and, at the insistence of her father, she went to church with her parents. The message that day was on trust. God provides us with the strength to serve Him. As we serve Him, our trust grows. Nothing happens without His permission. We must learn to trust the past to God's mercy, trust the present to His grace, and trust the future to His divine guidance. God is in control. She vowed right then to discuss her religious beliefs with her friend.

[1]1 John 2:17

"I was afraid you'd bring that up sooner or later," he said, when they went out on a date that evening. "I'm not comfortable talking about it, and you wouldn't want to hear the things I could tell you. We have great times together. Why ruin it with all that religious stuff?"

It isn't necessary to open up and expose your inner self to everyone you see. But if you claim to believe in God, there is no way you can hide it under a bushel. God works through you to develop your faith and trust in Him. As your faith and trust in Him grows, the way you behave changes. You cannot deny Him. God extends His golden scepter to all who seek Him. Why not reach out today and accept His invitation?

> *For Mordecai the Jew was next unto King Ahasuerus,*
> *and great among the Jews, and accepted of the*
> *multitude of his brethren, seeking the wealth*
> *of his people, and speaking peace to*
> *all his seed.*
> Esther 10:3

Suggested Scripture Reading

Book of Esther.

Study Questions

1. Mordecai was taking care of Esther. Where were her parents?

2. Esther was chosen to train for the king's harem. Why did she choose not to let anyone know she was a Jew?

3. Mordecai overheard two men plotting a murder. What was written in the king's chronicles about the incident?

4. Mordecai refused to honor Haman. Who was Haman?

5. The king wanted to honor Mordecai. What were the king's plans?

6. Mordecai insisted that Esther talk to the king. Why was Esther hesitant to do so?

7. Esther waited for the opportune time to expose Haman. How did she plan for this?

8. Haman built a gallows to hang Mordecai. How did the gallows end up being used?

9. Haman was a wealthy man. What happened to his wealth?

10. Mordecai, a Jew, worked outside the palace. How did he spend his later life?

Fig. 9. Ceremonial Cup.
Cups similar to this were common objects
found in the palaces of princes and kings
during the reign of Queen Esther.

Chapter 20

JONAH

∘————∘

But I say unto you, "That every idle word that
men shall speak, they shall give account
thereof in the day of judgment."
Matthew 12:36

J onah, an Israelite prophet, was the son of Amittai. He lived during the eighth century B.C. in Galilee. Although Jonah is mentioned in 2 Kings 14:25 as God's servant who prophesied Israel's
growth under King Jeroboam II (785 – 745 B.C.), the Book of Jonah
features him as one of the Minor Prophets of the Old Testament.

God sent Jonah on a mission to Nineveh, the capital of Assyria,
when that kingdom was threatening the Northern Kingdom, Israel.
Jonah was afraid Nineveh would repent and be spared, allowing
Nineveh to continue her cruel and blasphemous ways. God told
Jonah to turn the people from idolatry back to Him. Instead, Jonah
fled to Joppa and boarded a ship to Tarshish to escape the presence
of the Lord.

A great wind and storm came down on the ship. The frightened
crew cast lots to find out who caused the wrath. They determined it
was Jonah, who was asleep below. Upon questioning him, they found
out that he was fleeing from God.

The mariners asked Jonah what they should do to calm the sea.
He told them to cast him overboard. Reluctant to do this, the sailors
rowed hard to get to shore, but the storm worsened. The Lord had
prepared for a great fish to swallow Jonah when he was cast overboard. Jonah was in the belly of the fish for three days and three
nights. God's miracle kept him from being digested by the fish.

Jonah prayed while he was in the belly of the fish, giving thanks that he was saved from drowning. He voiced his terror in the grips of the ocean and promised to obey the Lord if he were saved from death. Jesus referred to Jonah's situation when He said, "For as Jonas was three days and three nights in the whale's belly, so shall the Son of man be three days and three nights in the heart of the earth."[1] As soon as Jonah acknowledged that salvation is of the Lord, the fish vomited him onto dry land.

The Lord spoke to Jonah the second time, telling him to go to Nineveh and preach to the people. It took Jonah three days to get to Nineveh, where he urged the people to repent or the city would be overthrown in forty days. The king ordered fasting and a return to God. The Ninevites were worshipers of Dagon, a fish god. They were aware of what happened to Jonah. Jonah, who showed no signs of having been ingested by the fish, was an omen to them, urging them to repent. God saw that they had repented and had mercy on them. Nineveh was spared—this time. History notes that the Assyrians reverted to their wickedness, and their capital was destroyed 150 years later.

Jonah was displeased that the Gentile enemies of Israel had been spared. He pointed out to God that he had tried to go to Tarshish because he knew God was merciful and kind and would handle the people of Nineveh. God asked Jonah if he felt it was right for him to be so angry. Jonah left the city and sat near the outskirts to witness the outcome of the city's repentance.

The Lord placed a large plant over Jonah to protect him from the sun. This pleased Jonah. However, the Lord sent a worm to eat on the plant and cause it to wither. When the sun came up, the heat and a strong wind caused Jonah to become uncomfortable and faint. He wished he were dead.

God questioned Jonah. He compared Jonah's pity on the dead, which he had done nothing to help grow, with the Lord's pity on the spiritual death of Nineveh, which had over 120,000 stray souls (not to mention an abundance of livestock). God had saved not just a favored few, but thousands.

Assyrian famines occurred in 765 and 759 B.C. These events, as well as a total eclipse in 763 B.C., were interpreted by the Ninevites as forewarnings from the Lord intended to jolt them out of their brief bout with false gods.

---

[1]Matthew 12:40

Jonah fled from the work God appointed him to do instead of bowing down in loving obedience. When God gives a command—as He did to Jonah—it is not a question of what God will do, but how we will respond to His command.

———

Ned held a responsible position with a leading finance company. He handled the accounts of some of the most influential citizens of the large city in which he lived. True, he seldom met them face-to-face, yet he was entrusted to be guardian of their interests for the sole purpose of netting an increase each quarter of the fiscal year. His superior respected Ned's honesty and his ability to oversee the fortunes of his clients.

Ned's family was proud of him too. His mother had given him a bronze plaque to keep on his desk: *The love of money is the root of all evil.* How appropriate for someone who managed millions of dollars as though he were counting the pennies he saved in his piggy bank as a youngster. She had taught him the value of honesty, obedience, and respect.

Ned sat staring at the balance sheet handed to him by his superior a few hours before, asking him to initial it and pass it on to his secretary for filing. To the average person, it appeared correct. To Ned's well-trained eye, it appeared incorrect. "I can't initial this, Sir. These figures misrepresent actual transactions for this quarter." He stood before the vice-president of the company.

"I did not request validation. I simply asked you to initial the report. I suggest you do as you are told," was the man's icy reply.

"I'm sorry, Sir. I cannot," replied Ned, placing the paper on the VPs desk. Ned turned and walked toward the door.

So often we read and study the Word of God. Yet we do not live according to it. The daily news is filled with reports of fraud, embezzlement, swindle—cheating by any other name is still evil. Whether it is corporate chicanery or dime-store duplicity, whether committed by a high-ranking official or a penniless pauper, evil is sinfulness. Only when we have the strength and inner courage to follow the law of the Lord will we receive His mercy and blessing.

The men of Nineveh shall rise in judgment with this generation,
and shall condemn it:because they repented at the preaching
of Jonas;and behold a greater than Jonas is here.
Matthew 12:41

Scripture Reading

2 Kings 14:25; Jonah 1 – 4; Matthew 12:39-41.

Study Questions

1. Jonah was a prophet of the Lord. Why did God send him to Nineveh?

2. Jonah went to Tarshish. Why did he disobey God?

3. Jonah thought the Ninevites would repent. Why was he opposed to that?

4. Jonah boarded the ship. Why did the crew throw him overboard?

5. Jonah spent three days inside the fish. Why did Jesus refer to this in Matthew 12?

6. The fish spit Jonah out. Why was Jonah saved from drowning?

7. The Lord sent Jonah to Nineveh. Why was he sent there?

8. The Ninevites repented. Why did God show mercy on them?

9. Jonah pouted and left the city. What did the Lord do to protect Jonah from the elements?

10. God questioned Jonah. How did God compare Jonah's pity with His own pity?

Chapter 21

JOSEPH FATHER OF JESUS

And Jacob begat Joseph the husband of Mary,
of whom was born Jesus, who is called Christ.
Matthew 1:16

There are more than a dozen men of Biblical prominence named Joseph mentioned in the Old and New Testaments. Joseph, the father of Jesus, is listed as the son of Jacob in Matthew 1:16 and the son of Heli in Luke 3:23. He is called the husband of Mary in Matthew 1:16 and the father of Jesus in Luke 4:22, John 1:45, and John 6:42. A misconception is that he was an older man. This assumption may be because he is not mentioned in the Scriptural accounts of the mature Jesus. He was considered a righteous man because he would not willingly humiliate his pregnant wife-to-be. Although the Luke 1:26-80 account of Joseph, a carpenter, and Mary, a virgin, is more familiar, the story is also found in Matthew 1:16-25.

During the era of Mary and Joseph, a betrothal was a form of engagement as we understand it today, but more binding. A betrothal could be broken only by divorce. Unfaithfulness before the marriage ceremony was considered adultery, which was punishable by death. When Mary became pregnant during her betrothal to Joseph, naturally a cloud of suspicion hung over her. There had never been a virgin birth, so people assumed that a pregnant, unwed woman had committed adultery.

While Joseph was considering what to do, the angel of the Lord appeared to him in a dream saying, "Joseph, thou son of David, fear not to take unto thee, Mary thy wife:for that which is conceived in her is of the Holy Ghost."[1] All of this had been prophesied:"Behold a virgin shall conceive, and bear a son, and shall call his name Immanuel," which means 'God with us'.[2]

Joseph awoke from his dream and did as the angel of the Lord told him to do and took Mary as his wife.(They were not intimate until after the birth of her firstborn whom they named Jesus.)

Joseph and Mary went to Bethlehem to pay their taxes. Mary was great with child. It was there, in a manger, that Jesus was born. When Jesus was eight days old, Joseph and Mary took Him to the Temple, where He was circumcised and officially named Jesus. Shortly thereafter, Joseph planned to return to Nazareth with his family.

Joseph was visited again in a dream by the angel of the Lord, telling him to flee with his family to Egypt because Herod was looking for the Child whom he planned to destroy. Joseph complied and stayed there until Herod died.

After Herod's death, the angel of the Lord appeared in a dream to Joseph and told him it was safe for him and his family to leave Egypt and return to Israel. However, when Joseph learned that Herod's son was reigning, he took his family to Galilee and settled them in Nazareth. That way, he was fulfilling the prophecy that said the Messiah shall be called a Nazarene.

Mary and Joseph traveled to Jerusalem every year at the feast of the Passover. When Jesus was twelve years old, He lagged behind, unbeknownst to His parents, staying in Jerusalem when they began their journey back to Nazareth. They found Him three days later in the Temple, listening to and asking questions of the elders. He returned with them to Nazareth and obeyed them as children were expected to obey and respect their parents.

Jesus was remembered as being the son of Joseph when He began teaching and amazing his listeners. Joseph is mentioned two more times as the father of Jesus.[3]

Often we need reassurance and guidance when our lives become complicated. Joseph was a caring person. He did not want to embarrass Mary. He was more interested in her welfare than in his own.

---

[1]Matthew 1:20, [2]Isaiah 7:14, [3]John 1:45; 6:42

The sign in the front yard said the woman could foretell the future. The temptation was too strong for Maria. She could not control her impatience. She wanted to know right now. Should she tell John she was pregnant? Would he marry her if he knew? Or should she coax him into marrying her and then tell him?

Maria and John were engaged. They were waiting until John graduated from college next year before they wed. They broke one of God's laws during Christmas break. Now she was considering yielding to temptation by seeking the advice of a soothsayer. How would John react to this?

The temptation was too much. Maria knocked on the door of the small frame house and was asked to enter the candle-lit room. The older woman, who was dressed in a loosely fitted long dress and wearing a turban-like scarf on her head, motioned for Maria to sit in the empty chair at the round table. The smell of burning incense increased the nagging nausea in Maria's stomach.

The woman told her in a convincing tone of voice that her future was bright.... She saw a new face in her future.... She had some tough decisions to make.... A new life was before her.... She should not delay.... On and on went the noncommittal, ambiguous barrage of verbiage. The session lasted thirty minutes and cost Maria fifty dollars. Maria gasped for air as she headed for her car. The nausea was overtaking her.

She did not see the tree limb protruding from the back of the truck that made a left turn as she stepped around to her car door. When she awakened, she was lying in a hospital bed. There was her mother, listening to the doctor, who said, "She'll experience cramps and some bleeding...."

However painful it was, Maria learned a valuable lesson. God forgives us our sins when we confess them to Him. But we pay the consequences. We do not always understand why God allows some things to occur. It is not necessary for us to understand. We do not see the whole picture as God sees it, nor does anyone else on this earth. We must accept the fact that God is in control, that His timing is best, and that we must put our trust in Him.

And Jesus himself began to be about thirty years of age,
being (as was supposed) the son of Joseph,
which was the son of Heli.
Luke 3:23

Scripture Reading

Matthew 1:16-24; 2:13; Luke 1:26-80; 2:4, 16, 33, 43; 4:22; John 1:45; 6:42.

Study Questions

1. Joseph was a carpenter. What was his reaction when he found out Mary was with child?

2. Joseph was betrothed to Mary. How did a betrothal at that time differ from an engagement in today's society?

3. Mary was pregnant. How did those around her react to her pregnancy?

4. Joseph was considering a divorce. Why did he change his mind?

5. Mary's time was near. Why were she and Joseph traveling?

6. Joseph paid his taxes. Why did the family not return home?

7. Joseph and Mary traveled to Jerusalem each year. Why did they go?

8. Jesus was separated from His family in Jerusalem. Where did they find Him?

9. Joseph was not an old man. Why is it sometimes thought he was older when he was betrothed to Mary?

10. Jesus was of the lineage of David. How is His lineage traced?

Fig. 10. Wooden Toy.
Dating 1st – 2nd Century A. D., found in Israel.
A similar handmade wooden toy was likely the
type of toy Joseph made for Jesus.

Chapter 22

SIMEON

*And, behold, there was a man in Jerusalem, whose name
was Simeon: and the same man was just and devout,
waiting for the consolation of Israel: and the
Holy Ghost was upon him.*
Luke 2:25

Simeon was waiting for the coming of the Messiah. He had been promised by the Holy Spirit that he would see the Messiah before he died. Mary and Joseph came to the Temple forty days after Jesus' birth for Mary's purification ceremony. It was during this ritual that Simeon entered the area of the Temple where Mary and Joseph stood with the infant Jesus. Simeon took Jesus in his arms and uttered his memorable words:"Lord, now lettest thou thy servant depart in peace, according to thy word:for mine eyes have seen thy salvation. Which thou hast prepared before the face of all people:A light to lighten the Gentiles, and the glory of thy people Israel."[1]

After his outburst of praise to God, Simeon spoke prophetically to Mary, telling her that Jesus was destined "for the fall and rising again of many in Israel; and for a sign which will be spoken against; yea, a sword shall pierce through thy own soul also, that the thought of many hearts may be revealed."[2]

Simeon was simply saying that those who are too arrogant to believe and repent will fall and be punished. Those who fall to their knees, ask forgiveness, and receive Jesus into their hearts will be greatly blessed. The arrival of Jesus on earth was a threat against sin. His presence was going to bring out the ugliest impulses of the human race. Simeon predicted that Mary would witness Jesus'

[1]Luke 2:29-32, [2]Luke 2:34–35

crucifixion, filling her heart and the hearts of those who believed in Him with great sorrow.

The way we react to Jesus as Lord and Savior is a revelation of our true feelings. Simeon's brief words were accurate indicators of the future of the infant child in his arms, as well as the grief His mother and His followers would endure. He ended with the assurance of eternity for those who accept Jesus as their Lord and Savior.

⸻

It was the old man's birthday. He checked the telephone to make sure it was still working. He cleaned the coffee pot and set out two special cups and saucers—the ones his son had given to him many years ago for his birthday. His son would be pleased that his father still had them. His son always came to see him on his birthday.

The ringing of the telephone roused the old man from a nap. It was afternoon, and the cups were still on the table. His son must have been busy this morning. He was probably calling now. "No, ma'am, I don't watch television, so I can't help you with your survey." His disappointment showed in his wavering voice. Wiping away a tear, he hung up the phone.

"Train up a child in the way he should go, and when he is old he will not depart from it."[3] "He is a good son. Something happened or he would have come to see me on my birthday," the old man said to himself. The tears in his eyes distorted his vision as he reached up to put the cups back on the shelf. *Crash!* He would sweep up the broken pieces tomorrow.

We all have expectations. Without them, our faith would not grow. Through them, it is often strengthened. Only Jesus Christ can pick up the fragments and make us whole.

And it was revealed unto him by the Holy Ghost,
that he should not see death, before he
had seen the Lord's Christ.
Luke 2:26

---

[3]Proverbs 22:6

Scripture Reading

Luke 2:25-35.

Study Questions

1. Simeon was elderly. What had the Holy Spirit promised him?

2. Mary and Joseph came to the Temple. Why were they there?

3. Simeon held the infant Jesus. What did Simeon say?

4. Simeon praised God. What did he say to Mary?

5. Simeon spoke prophetically. What did he say in *lay* terms?

6. Simeon made a prediction. What did he say Mary would witness?

7. Simeon's words were future indicators. What two things did he say would have to be endured?

8. Simeon gave words of assurance. What was the assurance?

9. The Holy Spirit made Simeon a promise. How was the old man in the story like Simeon?

10. The old man's cups were broken. How does God deal with shattered lives?

Chapter 23

LAZARUS

⌒—⌒

*Jesus said unto her, "I am the resurrection, and the
life: he that believeth in me, though
he were dead, yet shall he live.*
John 11:25

In Luke 16:19-31, Jesus tells the parable of the rich man and Lazarus. It is uncertain whether this is the same Lazarus as the one in John 11–12. Although there is the connection of "rising from the dead", it is not explicit. The uncertainty does not end there. Sisters Mary and Martha are named both in Luke and John. But only in John are they identified as sisters of Lazarus, about whom this chapter is concerned.

Lazarus and his sisters, Mary and Martha, lived in Bethany. Lazarus became ill. Because he and his sisters were close friends of Jesus, the sisters sent word to Him, telling Him that Lazarus was sick.

When Jesus got the message, he was on the east side of the Jordan River. His response to them was, "this sickness is not unto death." The true significance of Lazarus' sickness was that God would be glorified through it. Jesus would be manifested as the true Messiah. Jesus remained there two more days before deciding to go to Judea. His disciples were concerned for Jesus' safety in Judea and were surprised that He would go there.

Jesus said to His disciples, "Our friend Lazarus sleepeth."[1] He was referring to death, but the disciples did not understand it that way. The disciples felt that sleep would be good for Lazarus since he was sick. Jesus said more clearly to them, "Lazarus is dead. And I am glad for your sakes that I was not there, to the intent ye may believe; nevertheless, let us go unto him."[2] Lazarus did not die because Jesus was angry with him or because of any sin he had committed.

---

[1]John 11:11, [2]John 11:15

When Jesus arrived in Bethany, about two miles from Jerusalem, Lazarus had been in his tomb for four days. Mary and Martha were surrounded by Jews who had come to comfort them. Martha heard that Jesus was on His way and went to meet Him. When they met, she again reminded Him that Lazarus would not have died had Jesus been with him. Jesus told her that her brother would rise again.

Martha understood this to mean that he would rise again in the Resurrection at the Last Day. Jesus questioned Martha about her belief. Although she really did not understand the implication of what Jesus said, she soon saw the light and confessed her belief that He was Christ, the Son of God.[3]

Martha went back to tell Mary that Jesus was asking for her. Mary went to meet Jesus. When the mourners saw her, they followed, thinking she was going to the tomb. Mary met Jesus and fell at His feet, saying, "Lord, if thou hadst been here, my brother had not died."[4]

Jesus saw Mary and all the mourners weeping and asked where Lazarus was buried. It is written, "Jesus wept."[5] They all realized how much Jesus loved Lazarus and questioned why He had not kept him from dying. Jesus wept in sorrow over the effect sin has on the entire human race. Those who witnessed His sorrow failed to understand that He loved them as well.

When Jesus approached the tomb, He told the mourners to take away the stone that sealed the tomb. He prayed first and then said in a loud voice, "Lazarus, come forth."[6] Lazarus came from the grave, bound in his grave clothes. Jesus told the mourners to remove the bindings so that Lazarus could walk freely. In the same way, it is up to us to remove the stumbling blocks and other obstacles that bind us in the throes of sin.

Seeing the miracle, many of the Jews believed in Him. Others went to tell the Pharisees what Jesus had done. "If we let him thus alone, all men will believe on him; and the Romans shall come and take away both our place and our nation."[7] Jesus continued His journey, walking and teaching among the people.

Six days later, Jesus had supper with Lazarus and his sisters. Mary anointed Jesus' feet with a very expensive ointment and wiped His feet with her hair. Judas complained that Mary should not have used the expensive ointment, but Jesus scolded him, saying, "For the

---

[3] John 11:27, [4]John 11:32, [5]John 11:35, [6]John 11:43, [7]John 11:48

poor always ye have with you; but me ye have not always."[8] We should take every opportunity to do all we can to magnify the Lord.

Many Jews came to see Lazarus. The chief priests considered that Lazarus, as well as Jesus, might be put to death. Those who spread the Word of God are often the target of persecution. When people heard Jesus was coming to Jerusalem the next day, they met Him. They waved palm branches and cried, "Hosanna:Blessed is the King of Israel that cometh in the name of the Lord."[9] Many of these same people were there when Jesus called Lazarus out of his grave. The disciples did not realize that they were witnessing the fulfillment of Zechariah's prophecy until after Jesus ascended into heaven to be glorified at the right hand of God.[10]

There is no further mention of Lazarus in the Scripture. This was the last great miracle of Jesus in His ministry.

The story of Lazarus is a profound instance where God's delays are not His denials. He is in control. His timing is best. We must keep with the Divine timetable. Mary and Martha, however painful it was for them, were taught a lesson on patience. We too will not be taken before God's appointed time as long as we do His will and walk in fellowship with Him.

<hr>

The story of Lazarus parallels the persecution of Jesus Christ. The persecution continues to this day in many parts of the world. Soon after the onset of 2005, a young pastor was beaten to death in India. His name was added to the growing list of martyrs there. The South India State of Kerala, where eighty-five percent of the population is Christian, continues to be plagued with persecution of Christians by militants. Following the death of the young pastor, another pastor and five Bible College students were severely beaten and hospitalized while preaching the Word of God in Kerala.

Bishu was thrown into jail for robbing and killing another man. He was so dangerous that he was chained to his bed. Joshu was thrown into the same jail for street-preaching. The jail was a dark, filthy pit unfit for human habitation. On the one hand, Bishu was an unfit human and seemingly deserved to be treated in such a way. Joshu, on the other hand, was following God's commandment to spread the Gospel.

[8]John 12:8, [9]John 12:13, [10]John 12:16

In the dank darkness of despair and evil, Joshu sat on Bishu's cot and told Bishu of God's loving care. Bishu, a murderer, was released from jail before Joshu, a witness for Jesus Christ. Bishu was so convinced by Joshu's testimony that he made up his mind to let the Lord use him. He began street-preaching, an intriguing yet awesome sight to his one-time friends.

A mob entered his house and demanded that he cease his preaching. Bishu offered them tea and invited them back the next day. The men returned. Bishu again spoke to them of his new God and His promise of eternal life. He offered them tea and invited them back the next day. They returned the next day but refused to sit down and listen to Bishu. They threatened to kill him if he continued to talk about this new God. Bishu showed them the scars on his neck, arms, and body, and said, "I received these wounds for being evil. The Lord Jesus Christ received similar wounds for being the Son of God. He is working through me to deliver you from evil." The men turned and walked away. Bishu never saw them again. Today he and Joshu are pasturing a church in a village in South India.

And whosoever liveth and believeth in me
shall never die. Believeth thou this?
John 11:26

Scripture Reading

John 11:1-48; 12:1-19.

Study Questions

1. Lazarus became ill. Why did his sisters send for Jesus?

2. Jesus was two miles away. Why did He not come immediately?

3. Jesus said that Lazarus was asleep. What did He mean?

4. Jesus said He was glad He was not with Lazarus. Why?

5. Jesus told Martha her brother would rise again. What did He mean?

6. Martha thought Jesus referred to the Last Day. When did she fully understand Him?

7. Jesus wept. Why did Jesus weep at Lazarus' tomb?

8. Jesus returned to Bethany. What took place at Lazarus' house?

9. Judas objected. Why did Jesus scold him?

10. The chief priests thought Lazarus would be put to death. Why?

Fig. 11. Roman Key.
1ST-3rd Century A.D. A twelve-inch iron key similar to those used
by the Romans.

Chapter 24

JOHN
THE BAPTIST

———

*And Jesus, when he was baptized, went up straightway out of the
water: And, lo, the heavens were opened unto him, and he saw the
Spirit of God descending like a dove, and lighting upon him:and lo a
voice from heaven, saying, This is my beloved Son, in whom
I am well pleased.*
Matthew 3:16-17

Zechariah was a priest. He had been chosen by lot to burn
incense in the Temple, a once in a lifetime priestly opportunity.
While he was performing his duty, an Angel of the Lord—
Gabriel—appeared. Zechariah was frightened and was left speechless.
It was at this time that Gabriel told him that his wife Elizabeth, though
elderly and barren, would conceive and bear a son whom Zechariah
would name John. The son would be great, filled with the Holy Spirit,
leading many people to God through repentance. The son became
known as John the Baptizer, forerunner of the Messiah.

Elizabeth secluded herself in her home for the next five months,
preparing for the birth of her son. At about the same time, Gabriel
appeared to Mary, telling her that God had chosen her to be the
mother of the long-awaited Messiah. He told her of her cousin
Elizabeth's pregnancy. Mary visited Elizabeth and stayed with her for
three months. When Elizabeth heard Mary's voice, the baby leaped
in her womb.[1]

---

[1] Luke 1:41

During the circumcision ceremony for Zechariah and Elizabeth's baby, the onlookers were surprised when Elizabeth announced that the baby's name would be John instead of being named for his father. John was six months older than Jesus.

John was characterized by his raiment of camel's hair and a leather belt. His diet was locusts and wild honey. His ministry encompassed the Wilderness of Judea and his message was "Repent for the kingdom of heaven is at hand."[2] People from all Judea gathered to hear him preach. Those who responded to his message were baptized in the Jordan River. John recognized that the Pharisees and Saducees who came were not sincere. He told them that those found unfit for heaven would "be cut down and thrown into fire" just as a fruitless tree is destroyed.

John explained that the water with which he baptized was ceremonial with no intrinsic cleansing power. Though their repentance was real, it did not offer them full salvation. The baptism with the Holy Spirit (God's blessing) and fire (His judgment on those who do not show true repentance) is the true baptism.

Jesus walked from Galilee to the lower Jordan River to be baptized by John. Jesus had no sins of which to repent. John felt Jesus should baptize him. Jesus answered, "Suffer it to be so now; for thus it becometh us to fulfill all righteousness."[3]

John's mission was to testify that Jesus was the true Light of the World. John was put into prison by King Herod. Jesus took this as an omen of His own demise. From that point on, He took up John's message—"Repent, for the kingdom of heaven is at hand."

John's stretch in prison was getting to him. He sent two of his disciples to question Jesus—to ascertain if He were the promised Messiah. Jesus sent word to John, reminding him of the miracles He had performed and the preaching He was doing, adding, "And blessed is he who is not offended because of me."[4] Jesus was reassuring John, not scolding him. Jesus praised John to the multitudes as a fearless prophet-like messenger of the Lord.[5]

Herod the Tetrarch (son of Herod the Great) left his wife for an adulterous relationship with his brother Philip's wife. John denounced him for his immorality. Subsequently, the king had John imprisoned.

On Herod's birthday, the daughter of the woman with whom he was involved danced for him so enticingly that he offered her anything

---

[2]Matthew 3:2, [3]Matthew 3:15, [4]Matthew 11:6, [5]Matthew 11:4-19

she desired. Her mother prompted her to ask for John the Baptizer's head on a platter. Her wish was granted. John's disciples gave him a proper burial and then told Jesus what had happened. Herod was continually haunted by his beastly behavior.

The account of John the Baptizer is found in Matthew through Acts. The accounts are similar, but details vary. Importance is placed on the fact that John recognized Jesus as greater than himself—One who baptizes not with water but with the Holy Spirit. John's effective ministry impacted throngs of people. He is portrayed as a prophet, preparing the way for the Messiah.

John the Baptizer can well be described as a man of God. He was a hard-worker, courageous, and a prophet. Even though John was a contemporary of Jesus Christ, he cautioned people that Jesus, not he, was the long-awaited Messiah. He sought no glory for himself but magnified God in his ministry to the people.

Tomas gave in to God's call to spread His Word to the people in the remote villages of India who had never heard of Jesus. He left the security of his home and family to face a life of persecution among the savageness of idolaters. They sometimes appeared as militants and insurgents masked by religious affiliations. More often than not, they have been supported by their country's government.

Tomas survived bloody beatings, skull-bashing, and imprisonments by his tormentors. He accepted the mission to care for all God's children—especially orphans, widows, and lepers. He established Bible colleges to prepare young people native to India to become missionaries all over their country. Their message, like John's, was:If you want to practice a religion, remain an idolater; if you want to become a Christian, accept Jesus Christ as your personal Lord and Savior. "Repent for the kingdom of God is at hand."

Tomas is honored by his country's president one day for his humanitarian work and exiled another day for street preaching. He has remained on his assailants' top ten list for much of his ministry. Whether he is served up on a platter or burned in his car, Tomas believes God has a Divine timetable. As long as God keeps him here, he will be a willing servant of Jesus Christ, his Lord and Savior, preaching and baptizing with water those who hear and "repent for the kingdom of God is at hand."

Verily I say unto you, "Among them that are born of women there hath not risen a greater than John the Baptist: notwithstanding he that is least in the kingdom of heaven is greater than he."
Matthew 11:11

Scripture Reading

For in-depth study read the Gospels, specifically Matthew 3, 14; Mark 1; Luke 1; John 1; Acts.

Study Questions

1. Zechariah was John's father. Why was he in the Temple?

2. Gabriel appeared. What did he tell John?

3. John was the forerunner of the Messiah. Why did he become known as the *baptizer?*

4. Mary visited Elizabeth. What are some of the things they had in common?

5. Elizabeth announced the baby's name. Why did Zechariah not announce it?

6. John had an active ministry. What was the theme of his ministry?

7. John baptized with water. What was the difference between baptism with water and with the Holy Spirit?

8. John baptized Jesus. Why was he hesitant?

9. Jesus took up John's message. What was the message and why did Jesus preach it?

10. John was beheaded. Who did it and why?

Fig. 12. Roman Pen.
Found in the Jerusalem area; 1 – 3rd Century A.D.
This type of pen and ink, made of lamp soot and other materials, was
used to write on papyrus or parchment. Only the best writers
used this instrument to write because of the expense.

Chapter 25

SILAS

And Judas and Silas, being prophets also themselves,
exhorted the brethren with many words,
and confirmed them.
Acts 15:32

Silas, sometimes referred to as Silvanus, was an associate of Paul. He was a leader in the early church and a teacher in Jerusalem. When Paul and Barnabas delivered the decrees drawn up by the Apostles and elders from the Jerusalem conference to the church in Antioch, Silas and Judas Barsabbas were sent with them. Silas became an influential leader in the Macedonian churches, remaining there when Paul left on other missions.

When the letter from Jerusalem was read in the church at Antioch, those people were greatly encouraged. It confirmed that they were saved by God as Gentiles and not by becoming Jews. Silas and Judas stayed in Antioch along with many others, preaching and teaching the Word of God. Before returning to Jerusalem, they attended meetings in Antioch for fellowship and support. Paul later asked Silas to travel with him on his missionary journeys through Syria and Cilicia. They strengthened the churches there and delivered the decrees drawn up at Jerusalem. Silas was of help to Paul in his travels because he also had Roman citizenship.

When the missionaries reached Philippi, where there was no synagogue, they found a group of women meeting by the riverside. One of the women, Lydia, was a seller of purple-dyed cloth. She had been baptized. She invited Silas, Paul, Luke, and Timothy to stay in her home as guests.

One day when the missionaries were going to the prayer meeting, they met a slave girl who had the spirit of divination. She was able to foretell the future and make other revelations because she was demon-possessed. She cried out to the missionaries, "These men are the servants of the Most High God, which show unto us the way of salvation."[1] Paul knew he could not accept the testimony of demons, but he felt sorry for the slave girl. In the name of Jesus Christ, he commanded the demon to come out of her. She was freed immediately and became a rational person.

The girl's masters complained because they were losing money brought in by her fortune-telling. They dragged Paul and Silas before the magistrates and brought false charges against them. Actually, they called them trouble-makers, upsetting the Roman way of life. The magistrates stripped Paul and Silas of their robes and gave the command for them to be beaten.

The two were jailed with instructions for the jailer to keep them secured. He put them in the inner prison and fastened their feet in stocks. Paul and Silas sang and prayed, praising God. An earthquake occurred during the night, which caused the prison doors to open and loosened the prisoners' chains.

When the jailer awoke and saw the jail wide open, he drew his sword to commit suicide rather than face the wrath of his superior. Paul assured him that all the prisoners were accounted for. The jailer was so overcome that he shouted, "Sirs, what must I do to be saved?"[2]

Paul answered, "Believe on the Lord Jesus Christ, and you will be saved, you and your household."[3] Paul and Silas talked with the jailer about Christ while he cleansed their wounds. He accepted Christ as his Lord and Savior and was baptized. The jailer brought Paul and Silas into his house. After listening to them, his entire household came to know the Lord.

The magistrates sent orders for the jailer to release Paul and Silas the next morning. Paul refused to leave. He and Silas were Roman citizens who had been beaten and tried unfairly. He insisted that the magistrates come and release them personally. The magistrates came and apologized but insisted that Paul and Silas should leave the city immediately upon their release. First the two missionaries stopped at Lydia's home to teach and encourage their followers. Then they bade them farewell and left Philippi.

---

[1]Acts 16:17, [2]Acts 16:30, [3]Acts 16:31

Paul and Silas traveled thirty-three miles to Amphipolis. In a few days, they traveled thirty miles to Apollonia and then thirty-seven miles to Thessalonica, where they preached the gospel at a Jewish synagogue for three weeks. Many of the Jews were convinced that the Messiah had to suffer and rise again from the dead and that Jesus was the long-awaited Messiah. These same people became Christian believers, along with many prominent women.

Some of the Jews were upset because of the conversions. They provoked a riot to ravage the house of Jason, where Paul and Silas had been staying. They dragged Jason and some other believers before the city officials for "turning the world upside down."[4] Paul and Silas were gone. Jason and the others were charged with plotting to overthrow Caesar and the Roman government in favor of another king—Jesus. They posted bail and were released.

The missionaries were sent by night to Berea, where they preached in the Jewish synagogue to many Jewish and Gentile believers. When they heard that more conversions were taking place, Jews from Thessalonica came to Berea to stir up trouble. Paul was sent on to Athens to avoid the confrontation, but Silas and Timothy remained in Berea. Paul sent for them to join him in Athens. However, Paul left Athens and journeyed to Corinth, where he became friends with Aquila and Priscilla.

Silas and Timothy joined him in Corinth, preaching there for about eighteen months. The last mentions of Silas in the Scripture are in 1 and 2 Thessalonians 1:1. In these verses, Paul includes Silas and Timothy in the salutations of his letters to the church of the Thessalonians. They were traveling with Paul at the time.

☙━━━❧

Earthquakes, storms, floods, tsunamis, and other catastrophic events are recorded in Biblical accounts as acts of God. The earthquake in Philippi was considered a miracle. Has God ceased to work miracles? We still experience the violence of natural disasters, such as the tsunami that hit Asia on December 26, 2004. Did we overlook the miracles?

The young mother stood gazing at the wall of water out on the ocean where her husband had gone earlier in his fishing boat. It did

---

[4]Acts 17:6

not occur to her to turn and run toward the mountains. And then it was too late. The angry wave snatched her baby from her arms. He was swallowed up and gone. She held onto the post her husband had sunk deep in the sand to moor his boat. It seemed an eternity before someone came along on a makeshift raft, wrenched her frozen hands from the post, and rowed her to a safer place.

A week later, her husband was carried into the same refuge on a stretcher. All they could do was stare at each other. How could she explain that his son, his shining light, was gone?

Lists of names of survivors began appearing. Families were reunited—hundreds with no place to start their lives over again; hundreds with the dead bodies of their loved ones. And then one day a baby was brought into the refugee tent. Eight families claimed he was their child. What would Solomon have done?

Three long months later, based on DNA testing, the baby was placed back in his mother's arms. The family was together again. Just how do you define 'miracle'?

And when Silas and Timotheus were come from Macedonia,
Paul was pressed in the spirit, and testified to the
Jews that Jesus was Christ.
Acts 18:5

Scripture Reading

Acts 15:22-35; 16:19-38; 17; 18; 2 Corinthians 1:19; 1 and 2 Thessalonians 1:1.

Study Questions

1. Silas was a teacher in Jerusalem. Why did he go with Paul to Antioch?

2. The decree was read in the church at Antioch. How did the people respond?

3. Silas remained in Antioch. Why did Paul contact him at a later time?

4. There was no synagogue in Philippi. What did the missionaries find there?

5. The slave girl testified for Jesus. Why could Paul not accept her testimony?

6. Paul and Silas were taken before the magistrates. What were the charges against them?

7. Paul and Silas were beaten and jailed. What did they do while they were in jail?

8. An earthquake caused the jail doors to open. Why did the prisoners not run away?

9. The jailer was greatly affected. How did he react to the earthquake?

10. Silas was a traveling companion of Paul. What was the purpose of their travels?

Chapter 26

CORNELIUS

Then remembered I the word of the Lord, how that he said,
John indeed baptized with water; but ye shall
be baptized with the Holy Ghost.
Acts 11:16

The initial efforts of the great ministries of the Apostles of the first century B.C. were to convert Jews to Christianity. In cases where the Jews rejected their teachings, they went elsewhere. Paul, for example, preached to the Gentiles. Cornelius, a Roman centurion whom Peter converted, was a model Gentile convert.

Cornelius was stationed in Caesarea with a Roman regiment. He was a devout, God-fearing man. He gave to the poor and prayed daily to God. One evening, Cornelius saw a vision. An angel of God approached him and called his name. Cornelius was afraid. He thought it was God calling. He answered, "What is it, Lord?"[1]

The angel told him that, because of his prayers and his contributions to the poor, God wanted him. Cornelius was instructed to send men to Joppa to locate Simon Peter, who was living by the sea at the time. Peter would then tell him what to do.

Cornelius sent two of his servants and a devout soldier to Joppa the next day. As the trio drew near to Peter's house, Peter went up on the roof to pray. He became very hungry and fell into a trance. He saw heaven opened and a sheet was let down by its four corners. It was filled with beasts, creeping things, and fowls. A voice told him to rise, kill, and eat. Peter refused. After his third refusal, the sheet returned to heaven.

[1]Acts 10:4

In the meantime, Cornelius' men arrived. They stood at the gate, asking for Peter. Peter went down to the men and introduced himself. The men stated their mission. Peter let them spend the night in his house. He and a group of men left with them the next morning to return to Caesarea and talk with Cornelius.

As Peter approached Caesarea, Cornelius met him, fell at his feet, and worshiped him. Peter told him to stand up. They began talking and went into Cornelius' house, where a crowd had gathered. Peter reminded the crowd that it was unlawful for a Jew to come into a Gentile house. However, God told him not to judge them as being untouchable. "I ask therefore, for what intent ye have sent for me?"[2]

Cornelius told Peter of the vision he had experienced. Now he was eager to hear what it was that God wanted him to hear. Peter admitted that up to that time he had believed God favored the nation of Israel. Now he realized that God was more interested in an honest, contrite heart than whether a person was a Jew or Gentile. Jesus Christ is Lord of all. Peter preached the good Word to them. The Gentiles received the Holy Spirit and were baptized.

Word got back to Judea that the Gentiles had received the Word of God. When Peter was confronted with the fact that he had preached to the Gentiles, he told them of his vision and all that had happened. He explained how the Holy Ghost fell on them as he began to speak. He remembered the Word of the Lord, "John indeed baptized with water; but ye shall be baptized with the Holy Ghost."[3]

After the crowd that challenged Peter's involvement with Cornelius heard Peter's account of what took place, they recognized God's part in it. Their objections turned to praise to God for granting the Gentiles repentance unto life.

Peter used this incident to remind the Pharisees that God intended for the Gentiles to hear the Word of the Gospel and believe.[4] God used Peter to open the door of faith to the Gentiles. Regardless of race or country of origin, all true believers in the Lord Jesus Christ are as one in Christian fellowship. When we look for differences, we focus on one another. When we look for unity, our focus is on God.

---

[2]Acts 10:29, [3]Acts 11:16, [4]Acts 15:7

The old man could see the spot of shade just ahead, a promise of a cool drink of water and an escape from the searing sun. He could barely make out the form of someone already at the well. Perhaps she would draw a pail of water for him. "My good woman," he began, "will you be so kind as to draw me some water? I thirst."

"You're not from these parts or you wouldn't be asking me, or, for that matter, you wouldn't be talking to me," she replied in a snarling yet suggestive tone of voice. "A little drink of water won't get you very far."

"It depends on the water," he answered slowly. "When we wash away our differences and look for our similarities, the water becomes living water. A sip of living water quenches our thirst forever."

"The heat's been too much for you, old man," she replied. Her voice was guarded yet full of pity. "My life is in ruins. Tell me where I can find your living water, and I'll trade you this pail for a cup of it." She suddenly laughed, pouring a pail of cool water over him.

God uses various ways to lead sinners to the Lord. The woman was wrapped up in her own misery. She focused on the differences between her situation and that of the old man. Only when she accepted their common need for living water was she willing to help him. "But whosoever drinketh of the water that I shall give him shall never thirst; but the water that I shall give him shall be in him a well of water springing up into everlasting life."[5]

And God, which knoweth the hearts, bare them witness, giving them the Holy Ghost, even as He did unto us.
Acts 15:8

Scripture Reading

Acts 10:1-48; Acts 11:1-18; Acts 15:5-8.

Study Questions

1. The Apostles had great ministries. What were their goals?

---

[5]John 4:14

2. Some Jews rejected their teachings. To whom did the apostles preach?

3. Cornelius had a vision. What did he see?

4. The angel gave him instructions. What was he to do?

5. His servants left the next day. Where were they going?

6. Peter lived by the sea. What was the meaning of his vision?

7. Cornelius' men arrived. What did they tell Peter?

8. Peter was hospitable. How did he welcome them?

9. Cornelius met Peter. Why was Peter disturbed by Cornelius' actions?

10. Peter spoke to the crowd in Cornelius' house. What did he tell them?

11. The men of Judea were upset. What had Peter done to upset them?

12. Peter talked to the Pharisees later. What did he remind them?

Fig. 13. Roman Bronze Mirror.
Mirror with bone handle, 1st – 3rd Century A.D.
Paul used the metaphor of a mirror to compare our
capability to see Christ in this world with how we
will see Him at the resurrection.

Chapter 27

TIMOTHY

*This charge I commit unto thee, son Timothy, according to
the prophecies which went before on thee, that thou
by them mightest war a good warfare.*
1 Timothy 1:18

Timothy (also referred to as Timotheous) traveled with Paul and Silas on their missions. He was an associate and great helper of Paul who called him "my beloved son," and "faithful in the Lord."[1] Paul lists Timothy in the prescripts of at least four of his letters. These letters, full of descriptions of church work, earnestly exhort faithfulness. They are referred to as 'pastoral epistles'. Throughout Paul's letters, he portrays Timothy as a trusted associate and his useful emissary.

It is necessary to read and study Paul's missionary travels to get a glimpse of Timothy, rather than trying to extrapolate Timothy from the Scripture for independent study. It is much simpler to follow Paul through his travels and trials, read the 'pastoral epistles', and then characterize Timothy as an eager, young, determined disciple.

Timothy learned the essentials of the Christian faith from his mother Eunice, who was Jewish, and his grandmother Lois. His mother had married a Gentile, and their son had not been circumcised. Timothy quite possibly was converted when Paul first visited Lystra. It was at this point in time that he was circumcised by Paul.

Paul, Silas, and Timothy delivered the decrees drawn up by the Apostles and elders at Jerusalem to the churches in the cities of Lycaonia, Phrygia, and Galatia. From there, they went to Trovas. The Holy Spirit forbade their going into Asia and Bithynia.

---
[1] 1 Corinthians 4:17

The three traveled inland to Philippi, the foremost city of that part of Macedonia. They encountered a group of women worshiping on the riverbank because there was no synagogue. One of the women was Lydia, a seller of purple-dyed cloth. She invited them to be guests in her house. On another day, Paul freed a slave girl of her demons. Her owners made up false testimony against Paul and Silas, who were arrested, beaten, and put in prison.

Paul gave Timothy the special responsibility to minister to the Thessalonians. He introduced Timothy to them as "our brother and God's servant in the gospel of Christ." Timothy's report to Paul when he joined him in Corinth was that he had good news. The Thessalonians remained steadfast in faith and love and longed to see Paul.[2]

Paul planned to send Timothy to Philippi, saying "I have no one like him, who will be genuinely anxious for your welfare."[3] He went on to say how Timothy is like a son with a father, serving with him in the ministry.

Timothy remained in Ephesus, and Paul traveled to Macedonia. He cautioned Timothy to teach the Word of God and to warn the people to beware of false teachers. The thrust of his teaching was to encourage the people to accept only the Word of God. He concentrated on inducing faith in their hearts because there was so much cult-like teaching going on.

Paul told him to concentrate on the great truths of the Christian faith. His overall assignment was to produce "charity out of a pure heart, and of a good conscience, and of faith unfeigned."[4] According to his teaching, 'love' referred to loving God, fellow believers, and the world in general. This love can only come from a pure heart, one with sincere faith in God. The false teachers to which Paul referred in his letter were those who tried to combine Judaism (law) and Christianity (grace).

Silas and Timothy remained in Berea, while Paul went on to Athens. He sent for them, but by the time they caught up with him, he was in Corinth. Timothy and Erastus were with Paul in Ephesus. He sent them ahead to Macedonia while he stayed in Asia for awhile. Timothy was with Paul in Rome during Paul's first imprisonment.

---

[2]1 Thessalonians 3:6, [3]Philippians 2:19-24, [4]1 Timothy 1:5

George knew he was special. As a child, he was able to sense discord on the playground, in the classroom, and at home. He learned that it was easier to turn a deaf ear than to become involved. Even so, he often was asked to settle a dispute over who was right and who was wrong. Quite naturally he followed in his father's footsteps and became a schoolteacher.

George had a frequent dream: God was calling him to go into the ministry. "Teaching school is a ministry," he would tell himself each morning after having the dream. He began teaching Sunday School, thinking that would put a stop to the dream. It only strengthened his desire to study the Scripture.

One day he received a telephone call from a friend of his father, asking him to come to his office for a friendly chat. After a particularly hectic day at school, George wanted to cancel the appointment but kept it out of respect for his father. He felt his father was pushing him to change vocations. George was offered a high-paying opportunity within the company. He would set up and administer the company's in-house training program. George eventually accepted the offer.

Twenty-five years later, he is a well-respected, sought-after specialist in his field. He kneels in prayer each night before he goes to bed and thanks God for His many blessings. Yet, at least once a week, he still has that same dream: God calling him to go out into the world and spread the Gospel.

Once God's call comes, it does not stop. Timothy received the call when he was young and yielded to God's call to service. Not only was he a teacher, but he was also taught by one of the great teachers of all time. As we thank God for the spiritual gifts He has given us, do we remind ourselves to use those gifts to magnify God or are we using them to satisfy ourselves?

And that from a child thou hast known the Holy Scriptures,
which are able to make thee wise unto salvation
through faith which is in Christ Jesus.
2 Timothy 3:15

Scripture Reading

Acts 16 – 20; Romans 16:21; 1 Corinthians 4:17; 16:10; 2
Corinthians 1:1, 19; Philippians 1:1; 2:19; 1 and 2 Timothy.

Study Questions

1. Timothy traveled with Paul. Why did Paul request Timothy as a travel companion?

2. Timothy is mentioned often in the Scriptures. Why should we study Paul's missionary travels?

3. Timothy accepted Jesus as his Savior. Who were his influential teachers?

4. Paul circumcised Timothy. Why did he feel it was necessary?

5. Timothy and Silas traveled with Paul. What was their first assignment?

6. Timothy traveled to Philippi. Where did he stay?

7. Paul left Timothy in Thessalonica. What was his responsibility there?

8. Timothy remained in Ephesus. What problems had the people encountered?

9. The Christian faith is based on great truths. How did Paul suggest Timothy teach this to the people in Ephesus?

10. Paul was imprisoned. Who was with him during his first imprisonment?

Fig. 14. Papyrus Fragment.
Letters to the churches would have had the appearance
of this papyrus fragment which is written in Greek.

Chapter 28

NICODEMUS

*Jesus answered and said unto him, "Verily, verily,
I say unto thee, except a man be born again,
he cannot see the Kingdom of God."*
John 3:3

Nicodemus was a Pharisee, that is, a ruler and teacher of the Jews. He came to talk with Jesus at night. He admitted to Jesus that his people knew that Jesus came from God because of the miracles He performed. Jesus answered, "Verily, verily, I say unto thee, except a man be born again, he cannot see the Kingdom of God."[1]

Nicodemus did not understand how an old man could be born again without reentering his mother's womb. Jesus told him that he must be born of water and of the spirit. Physical birth is a beginning but is not enough. There must be spiritual birth produced by the Holy Spirit. Nicodemus did not recognize that Jesus was (and is) God.

Israel was under the control of Rome. Nicodemus was looking for the Messiah to free his people. Jesus' answers to Nicodemus were over the Pharisee's head. He took everything Jesus said literally, making it impossible to understand.

Jesus used an analogy from nature—the wind. One can neither tell where the wind comes from nor where it is going. Yet it is there, controlled by God. Nicodemus still did not comprehend. Jesus told him that, as a teacher of Israel, he should know and understand these things which were taught in the Old Testament Scriptures.

Jesus used the Old Testament incident of the Israelites being bitten by serpents and dying. Yet the bitten Israelite who looked

---

[1] John 3:3

to the brass serpent on a pole was miraculously healed. The serpent, brass, and pole were symbolic of Christ, Judgment, and the Cross.

When the Pharisees and chief priests sent officers to bring Jesus to them, the officers came back without Him. Accusations and intimidations swirled among them. Nicodemus spoke up, "Doth our law judge any man, before it hear him, and know what he doeth?"[2] Nicodemus must have finally understood what Jesus meant and actually trusted Him. Being born again, his new faith gave him the courage to stand up to other Pharisees in defense of the Lord. They had not given Jesus a fair chance. Should they not hear His case before they judged Him?

Nicodemus' own people turned on him, questioning his knowledge of the Old Testament. "No prophet would come out of Galilee." They were wrong, of course; Jonah was from Galilee. During the burial of Jesus in the tomb of Joseph of Arimathea, Nicodemus came with a hundred pounds of myrrh and aloes to spread on the body in preparation for burial.

Nicodemus is mentioned only in the Gospel of John. He is significant in that he represents the learned Jewish community, which, even though it did not understand Jesus' teachings, respected Him. Nicodemus and Joseph of Arimathea are typical of those Christians— past, present, and future—who lack the strength to stand up in public and say, "I believe in Jesus Christ as my Lord and Savior."

———

Mitzi went to church every Sunday morning. She enjoyed the fun, food, and fellowship. She listened closely to the sermons, although she admitted she did not always understand what the preacher was talking about. She prayed and thanked God for endowing her with good looks and the ability to make friends easily. Both assets were important in her line of work. She was a hostess in a nightclub. Although she occasionally recognized club patrons, none of them acknowledged seeing her. Her circle of friends, like herself, attended regularly, listened intently, took communion, put money in the offering plate, and looked forward to the next Sunday.

---

[2]John 7:51

Calvin was a regular attendee at the traditional service. He was reared in a strict religious family. He was well-versed in the scripture, had been baptized, and tithed. Calvin listened to the sermons, inwardly criticizing the preacher for talking down to the congregation. He recited the Lord's Prayer when he prayed at bedtime and the few times he was asked to lead in prayer. Several people from his office attended the same church. They nodded to one another, made mental notes of who had not attended, and went their separate ways.

Outwardly, both Mitzi and Calvin appear to be Christians. Inwardly, they both believe they are Christians. They each represent a different segment of society. They are both missing key elements of what Jesus expects them to know. They would both benefit from studying the Holy Scripture, perhaps in a small group. Being baptized by water is an important step. Being born again through baptism by the Holy Spirit is the giant step that gives us the courage to stand up and say, "I believe in Jesus as my personal Lord and Savior."

For God so loved the world, that he gave his only begotten Son,
that whosoever believeth in him should not perish,
but have everlasting life.
John 3:16

Scripture Reading

John 3; John 7; John 19:39.

Study Questions

1. Nicodemus was a Pharisee. What were his credentials?

2. He came to Jesus at night. Why?

3. His people knew that Jesus came from God. What did they not understand?

4. Jesus used analogies. Why did He expect Nicodemus to understand?

5. The Pharisees sent for Jesus. Why did they come back without Him?

6. Nicodemus defended Jesus. What did he say?

7. Nicodemus finally understood Jesus. What gave him renewed courage?

8. Jesus was crucified. What burial preparations were made?

9. Nicodemus is not mentioned after Jesus' burial. Why is his story significant?

10. Nicodemus believed in Jesus. What characterizes the type of people represented by Nicodemus and Joseph?

Fig. 15. Red Slip Pottery Shard.
2nd Century A.D. moulded design of a philosopher.
This redware plaque fragment of a philosopher is reminiscent
of Paul's speech to the people of Athens where he
likely encountered the best minds of the city.

Chapter 29

AQUILA

—◦◦—

Greet Priscilla and Aquila, my helpers in Christ Jesus:
who have for my life laid down their own necks:
unto whom not only I give thanks, but also
all the churches of the Gentiles.
Romans 16:3-4

Aquila was a Christian acquaintance of Paul. When Paul came to Corinth from Athens, he met Aquila, a Jew, and his wife Priscilla. Aquila was born in Pontus. He had recently come from Italy because of the edict by Claudius to expel all Jews from Rome. Paul stayed with Aquila and Priscilla. They were all tentmakers by occupation. They apparently had the financial means to travel and to maintain a household.

Paul left Corinth to minister in Syria. Aquila and Priscilla went with him. In Ephesus, they ministered to the Jews. They remained in Ephesus when Paul went on to Antioch.

An eloquent Jewish speaker named Apollos came to Ephesus. He spoke boldly and fervently in the synagogue. His problem was that he knew little about the teachings of Jesus other than baptism by water.

Aquila and Priscilla took him under their care and coached him in the way of God. Apollos became an acclaimed speaker, teaching that Jesus was the Christ, according to the scriptures.

Paul, in his letter from Corinth, gives recognition to those who have supported him in his ministry. He sends greetings to Aquila and Priscilla, who labor with him to bring others to Christ. He also mentions the church that they have in their house.

In Paul's letter from Ephesus, he again commends Aquila and Priscilla for their devotion and ministry in Ephesus. It was common at that time for Christians to gather in private homes for study, to worship, and to hear the word of God. Paul made the same request in his second letter to Timothy, which he wrote from prison in Rome.[1] Aquila's appearance in the scriptures is brief. Nevertheless, his lifestyle is one Christians today should emulate. Just as Aquila and Priscilla had a purposeful life, we too are here for a purpose. May we use it to magnify the Lord.

The old man was still living in the small hut where he was born and grew up. He reared his family there and expected his oldest son to move in when he passed away. He was highly respected in the village and was often consulted when there were problems. His home was open to anyone needing help or wanting the feeling of security in the presence of a confidant who was willing to listen.

The old man was shocked when the village police came to his hut. They informed him that his son had been arrested for dealing in drugs and stealing. His son—his eldest, the one who would carry on his name—had ceded to temptation. He listened in disbelief. To add to his consternation, the police wanted to search his hut for evidence.

Word soon circulated in the small village. No one came to the old man's hut anymore. He was shunned in the marketplace. He was being punished for the indiscretions of his beloved son. He was not even allowed to talk with him. His son did not wish to face his father.

The elderly priest decided something must be done. With the exception of the old man, he called the villagers to the temple for a special service. He mustered up all the pomp and ritual within his disposal. Although he had never seen nor heard of the Holy Scripture, his message was much like that of Jesus:"Let he who is without guilt cast the first stone." When he finished, there was much weeping and lamenting in that crowded temple. The villagers longed to embrace the old man and ask his forgiveness.

As the priest and a select group of villagers approached the old man's hut, they sensed that all was not well. He did not answer their knock on his door. The priest sent one of the flock to notify the

---

[1] 2 Timothy 4:19

authorities. On his own authority, the priest pushed open the door and entered. In the dimness, he could barely make out the outline of the old man slumped on the floor, as cold as the ashes in front of the crude fireplace. "Reproach hath broken my heart; and I am full of heaviness; and I looked for some to take pity, but there was none; and for comforters, but I found none."[2] God can mend a broken heart. But first He needs all the pieces.

Aquila and Priscilla are examples of the way Christians should live. They were hospitable, friendly, and generous. They made study and fellowship a part of their everyday life by establishing a church in their home and tutoring others to go out and preach the Gospel.

The churches of Asia salute you. Aquila and Priscilla salute you much in the Lord, with the church that is in their house.
1 Corinthians 16:19

Scripture Reading

Acts 18:2, 18, 26; Romans 16:3; 1 Corinthians 16:19; 2 Timothy 4:19.

Study Questions

1. Aquila was living in Corinth. Why was he living there?

2. Aquila met Paul in Corinth. What did they have in common?

3. Aquila accompanied Paul. How was he able to do this?

4. Aquila traveled considerably. Where did he go?

---

[2]Psalm 69:20

5. Aquila and Priscilla had a church in their house. Who was Apollos?

6. Aquila and Priscilla ministered to the Jews. How did they help Apollos?

7. Aquila set an example for Christian living. What were the key elements?

8. The old man had not heard of Jesus. Yet in what ways was he living according to the teachings of Jesus?

9. The old man was betrayed by his son. How would you react in a similar situation?

10. God can mend a broken heart. What must we do to receive His help?

Chapter 30

STEPHEN

*But he, being full of the Holy Ghost, looked up steadfastly
into heaven, and saw the glory of God, and
Jesus, standing on the right hand of God.*
Acts 7:55

A s the early Christian movement grew, it was inevitable that it
would collide with government authorities and religious
leaders. The people were expected to obey the law and to
show respect to their leaders. However, if a conflict arose between
manmade laws and God's laws, Christians were expected to disobey
secular law and suffer the consequences.

Stephen was a leader of the Jerusalem church. A dispute developed in the Jerusalem church between the Jewish Christians and the
Palestinian Christians. The Jewish (Grecian) widows were not receiv-
ing as much financial aid as the Hebrew widows. The Twelve
Apostles decided that the situation should be corrected. They did not
want to be involved in the financial matters of the church, so they
suggested that the church appoint seven men to take care of the matter. Stephen and Philip were among the seven Jewish Christians who
were chosen. Stephen was bold, wise, and full of faith.

The Apostles then could spend their time in prayer and the
ministry of the Word. They prayed and laid hands on the chosen
seven. Stephen, filled by the Spirit, was used by God to perform miracles and to preach God's word. The power of the Spirit led him to
confront his fellow Jews who did not believe Jesus was the Messiah.
Stephen reasoned that with Jesus as the Messiah, the Temple religion
was no longer useful. He felt that the Mosaic law should be re-inter-
preted.

Opposition to Stephen rose in the Synagogue. These Jews secretly induced false witnesses to accuse Stephen of blasphemy against Moses and God. He was misquoted as saying that Jesus would destroy the Temple and change that which Moses delivered to Israel.

During the trial, his accusers sat staring at Stephen. When they heard the charges against him, they saw the face of an angel, not the demon he was accused of being. The high priest asked Stephen if these things of which he was being accused were so. Stephen began his defense by reciting historical events, beginning with Joseph and Moses, who were raised up by God. He blamed Israel's leaders for killing Jesus and failing to follow God's law. At the same time, he reiterated his love for Israel.

Stephen was charged with speaking against the Temple. He skillfully turned the tables on his accusers, pointing out their guilt. This infuriated them. His words were God's last words to the Jewish nation. From this point forward, the gospel was directed toward the Gentiles.

Stephen looked toward heaven and said, "Behold, I see the heavens opened, and the Son of man standing on the right hand of God."[1] The crowd refused to hear anymore. They dragged Stephen outside the city walls and stoned him. As he was dying, he prayed, "Lord Jesus, receive my spirit. Lord, lay not this sin to their charge."[2] His body died, but his soul went to be with Christ. He was buried by a group of devout men who mourned greatly over him.

The death of Stephen parallels the death of Jesus in that they both were filled with the Holy Spirit. They both died unjustly. They both died uttering words of forgiveness. After Stephen's death, his fellow Messianic Christians scattered to other parts. He is referred to in Acts 11:19 and 22:20.

Lyra was a teacher who was dearly loved by her students. She planned activities that illustrated her lessons yet were enjoyable to the class. They looked forward to each day. Students who had done poorly in other classes excelled in Lyra's class. Her year-end test scores exceeded all other classes. She was acclaimed a model teacher, and her classes were used as demonstration classes for teaching "to succeed."

[1]Acts 7:56, [2]Acts 7:59-60

Her colleagues were jealous. They worked just as hard and were often given the problem students so that Lyra's classes would not be disrupted when observers were present. A former student confided that Lyra helped her cheat on the end-of-the-year achievement test. Another told that Lyra erased her wrong answers and penciled in the correct answer. As more and more reports filtered in, school officials decided to do an investigation to clear Lyra's name. Careful examination of the test papers, however, indicated that answers had in fact been altered. Lyra denied any wrong-doing.

Her class the next year still enjoyed her creative teaching style. However, year-end test results that year were no higher for her class than for the other classes. Claiming discrimination, Lyra asked for a transfer to another school. Sometimes we may stumble over the truth. When that happens, the only thing to do is to pick ourselves up and watch where we are going. When we walk by an untruth, we approve it. Jesus said, "I am the way, the truth, and the life; no man cometh unto the Father, but by me."[3]

And he kneeled down, and cried with a loud voice,
Lord lay not this sin to their charge. And
when he had said this, he fell asleep.
Acts 7:60

Scripture Reading

Acts 6:1 – 8:3; 11:19; 22:20.

Study Questions

1. Early Christians were expected to obey the law. What did they do when the law conflicted with their beliefs?

2. Stephen was a church leader. What dispute arose in his church?

---

[3]John 14:6

3. The church had twelve apostles. Why did they not settle the dispute?

4. Seven men were chosen. Why was Stephen chosen?

5. Stephen was filled by the Spirit. How did his teachings conflict with the beliefs of his fellow Jews?

6. Opposition rose in the Synagogue. What was Stephen accused of doing?

7. The accusers stared at Stephen. What did they see?

8. Stephen spoke in his own defense. On what did he base his defense?

9. Stephen looked toward Heaven. What did he see?

10. Stephen was stoned to death. What were his last words?

FROM THE AUTHOR

Studying the Holy Scripture is a never-ending joy. The information gained is invaluable in my work with women's groups, Sunday school, and study groups. Writing about the women of the Bible jarred the door wide open for other potential books, specifically one concentrating on the men of the Bible. The book is not intended to be all-inclusive nor were the thirty men chosen considered more important than those not included. In fact, there is so much information on some of the men that entire books have been written about the role they played in God's divine plan.

The Bible is a treasure trove of information, a prospectus of life. As we apply God's teachings to our lives, may we always remember that if we wish to find treasures, we must dig for them.

Praise be to God. Great things He has done!

For where your treasure is,
there will your heart be also.
Matthew 6:21

Illustrations

Figures 1–15 are photographs of original objects in The Arnold O. and Faith L. Guy Memorial Gallery and private collections, located in Lindenwood Christian Church, Memphis, TN. The focus of the teaching Gallery is to bring the Bible to life through archaeology and art. This material is used by permission of the Rev. Owen Guy, who established and maintains the collection, part of Lindenwood's Resource Center. *Men of God* is dedicated to Rev. Guy for his contributions of time and materials to enhance *Men of God*.

Titles by Nina P. Ross

God Will Provide
M.A. Thomas, *a biography*
ISBN: 0-9668796-0-0 hardcover; 0-9668786-1-9 softcover

God At His Best
A Mission Challenge, *a biography*
ISBN: 0-9668796-3-5; hardcover; 0-9668796-4-3 softcover

Beloved of God
the story of Ammini Cherian Thomas
as told by M.A. Thomas
ISBN: 0-9668796-2-7 softcover

Man of God
M.A. Thomas
ISBN: 0-9668796-6-X

All God's Children
Orphans and Lepers
ISBN: 0-9668796-5-1

Women of God
ISBN:0-9668796-7-8 hardcover;
0-96668796-8-6 softcover

Index